More

Reason to

Know

Him

By: Julie Coveney

ISBN: 9798640992236

Forward

There are moments in life when you come upon someone that walks in an unusual peace, and you are keenly aware that this peace must have been wrought by great pain. Julie is one such person.

I met Julie several years ago, and it was her peace that drew me to her. After hearing her story, I realized it was the surprise diagnosis of MRKH that brought this pain.

With great testament to Julie's faith and resilience, she has not allowed it to define her or envelope her very being. Instead, she has risen above this medical diagnosis by leaning into the One that created her, Jesus Christ.

If you have been diagnosed with MRKH - or any medical diagnosis - this book will bring you encouragement and point you to the One who can bring you hope. Julie's heart is for you, dear reader, to know that you are not alone. *More Reason to Know Him* provides resources to a vast community of support and encouragement. As you read this book, perhaps you will see some of yourself in Julie's story.

Now, get cozy, grab a cup of coffee or tea, and delve into this marvelous book.

Pastor Julia Mateer
Director of Groups, Bayside Community Church
Author of *Life-Giving Leadership: A Woman's Toolbox for Leading*

Praises for *More Reason to Know Him*

I'm proud of Julie for sharing her life story in, *More Reason to Know Him*. Many people go through tragic circumstances that make them bitter; causing them to live as victims the rest of their lives. Julie has shown that she's a victor, not a victim. Her story is told through tears, pain, happiness, and sorrow, but the overshadowing theme is joy. Her faith in a loving, heavenly Father, and her choice to see what life has given her instead of what it didn't, will encourage everyone.

Brenda Beattie
Author of *Finding Sacred Ground in the Daily Grind*

Julie's pain brings hope. You'll experience the love and acceptance she received and offers you as you journey through her book. Her story reminds me of the scripture, *"Praise be to the God and Father of our Lord Jesus Christ, the Father of compassion and the God of all comfort, who comforts us in all our troubles, so that we can comfort those in any trouble with the comfort we ourselves receive from God"* (2 Cor. 1:3-4 NIV).

Gloria Brush
Bible Study Leader, Bayside Community Church

A beautiful personal story of Julie's journey from 19 years old to the present. Feeling alone in her diagnosis of MRKH, Julie discovers she's not alone after all. God has been with her all along. After years of silence Julie's testimony brings much healing and freedom as she shares her MRKH with others. Meeting her MRKH sisters is a wonderful part of her story. You'll witness God's blessing of children and grandchildren via marriage, and children in Africa through a mission trip.

Denise Varga
Author of *Your Words Not Mine*

DEDICATION

More Reason to Know Him is dedicated to
my Lord and Savior, Jesus Christ.

Dedicated to my MRKH sisters, doctors and others to bring knowledge and awareness of Mayer, Rotikansky, Kuster, Hauser Syndrome, aka MRKH.

To my beautiful daughters, Lori and Kim, who made me a mom and grandma, and to my grandchildren: Ashley, James, Brianna, Jack, and Michael, for your love and understanding. You are all a blessing in my life! To my daughter's birth mom, Barbara, thank you.

To our daughter of the heart in Africa, Talent, and her son Lionel, thank you for all your love and prayers.

In memory of Meredith Brookes, the first MRKH sister I met. Meredith connected me with my MRKH sisters at my first meet-up in Philadelphia in 2016. You are missed. Thank you for your great work with MRKH.

Dedicated to all MRKH sisters around the world, you are amazing, strong, and beautiful. Thank you for all you've taught me on-line and at meetings. You are overcomers.

ACKNOWLEDGMENTS

To my husband, Terry, thank you for your lifetime support and understanding and for helping me through the highs and lows of coping with MRKH. I love how you encourage me no matter what. I especially appreciate your sense of humor that keeps me positive and laughing. I love doing life with you! You are my husband, best friend, life coach, and more.

Barbara Alpert is a fantastic writing mentor. Without her, this book would not be possible. Her professionalism, technical ability, and creative process in formatting this book are top-notch.

Thank you editors: Terry Coveney, Gloria Brush, Elaine Creasman. Your attention to detail and excellence is greatly appreciated.

Prayer Partners: Doretha Brown, Lori Bauer and Kim Guilford, Barbara Darks, Mary Jane Holleran, Joe Rosasco, JoAnn Rosell, Ellen Stem, Ann Black, Rosemary Smith, Tina Chila, and Talent. Thank you for your transformative gift of prayers to complete, *More Reason to Know Him.*

Groups Leadership Team: Pastor Julia Mateer, Pastor Dave Wilson, Isa Skuba, and Kaye Hurta. Thanks for prayers, good wishes, and send off to Australia.

Bible Study Groups/Prayer Partners: Dave and Barbara Murphy's group, Pastors Lou and Jean Judd's group, Gloria Brush's group. Cindy Wollard's group.

Missionaries: Pastor David and Annette Dann: Christ's Victory International - Liberia Africa. Don and Vera Bergson - South American Missions, Brazil.

INTRODUCTION

At 19 years of age, my life came to a screeching halt. I was a freshman in college, engaged to be married, and had a promising future. However, everything changed when I was diagnosed with MRKH. This syndrome got its name from the initials of the doctors that named it: Mayer, Rotakanski, Kuster, Hauser. Sadly, MRKH ended my engagement and dreams of having children and a family. The result was a lifetime sentence of infertility. I was covered in a state of deep darkness that was unchangeable!

MRKH is a rare disorder characterized by the failure of a uterus to develop fully when a child is in her mother's womb. A woman's failure to begin her menstrual cycle during puberty is a sign of MRKH. This condition happens to 1 in 5000 women. There is no known cause.

Because MRKH is rare, it is often not spoken about by many women who have it. A difficult diagnosis to receive, women with MRKH grieve the children they'll never have; especially when longing for motherhood. Although there is no way to understand being born like this, feelings of shame and secrecy accompany other emotions with MRKH.

As this story unfolds, I'll share how MRKH affected my life, and the various coping strategies I employed to survive. This comes from 50 years of living with MRKH, which did not include computers, counseling, cell phones, or doctor awareness.

Thankfully, today technology and increased awareness are available for MRKH women to navigate through their own personal journeys. Women with MRKH can have children by in-vitro fertilization/surrogacy or adoption. Uterine transplant is recent, and there have not been many as of yet. However, there have been successful uterine transplants; whereby MRKH women have carried a child and gave birth.

Learning about MRKH in 1970, caused me to title this book *More Reason to Know Him* because, God, was the only one I could share my diagnosis with and survive day-to-day living. He was with me then and is with me every step of the way. As challenging as my journey has been, I'm sharing my MRKH story—with all its lows and highs—to offer others hope and encouragement.

Today, after much healing and witnessing God's handiwork throughout my life, I consider MRKH a miraculous blessing! As strange as that may sound, I am thankful and wouldn't trade what it brought into my life.

Thank you, my MRKH sisters and other readers, for picking up this book. May God bless you immeasurably more as you read through its pages for whatsoever is your particular: *More Reason to Know Him.*

> *Hope deferred makes the heart sick,*
> *but a longing fulfilled is a tree of life.*

Proverbs 13:12 NIV

CONTENTS

The best and most beautiful things in this world cannot be seen or even heard but must be felt with the heart.

— Helen Keller

1

NEW BEGINNINGS

Did you ever go through life and feel excluded, unaccepted, invisible, or different from everyone else? As a young, quiet and shy girl, I often experienced these feelings growing up. Then, at age 19, I learned that I was actually different.

Journey with me and discover the ways I dealt with the devastating hand that was given me. Although it was difficult and isolating, I tried various coping strategies until my life changed for the better in 2003, which I will share with you as my story unfolds. First, let me tell you a bit about my family.

My five siblings were outgoing. Dad, very personable, was a liquor salesperson, and Mom was a homemaker. Mom was shy. Our oldest sister, Barbara, and our older brother, Al, were like a second set of parents. They were 10 and 8 years older than me. They were quite helpful to my parents with the rest of us. They had a busy childhood. I, for one, am glad Barbara and Al were so loving in how they cared for us.

Mom and Dad were verbally combative with each other. As individuals, my parents were great, but there was disharmony between them as a married couple. Having six children probably wasn't easy for them. Considering the circumstances, they did a good job raising all of us. Most of us attended Catholic school, from Kindergarten to 12th grade. The cost of tuition alone could have caused stress for them. The spirit of division permeated our family for years, unfortunately.

Alcoholism was a generational disease on both sides of my parent's families. We weren't perfect, that's for sure. Yet, I wouldn't trade my life for anything because it molded me and shaped me to be who I am today. I love my family, am grateful for my parents, and see the struggles many of us had related to alcohol at certain times of our lives. I genuinely believe it is an illness, and the cure is abstinence. Mom and Dad both had difficulty with alcohol. Eventually, Mom stopped drinking. For Dad, his health was greatly affected.

There were days where Mom and Dad were not under the influence of alcohol. We loved when that happened. My parents were beautiful, fun-loving people. Both had wonderful personalities. Dad loved to play golf with my brothers. Mom enjoyed tap dancing around the house while working. She was good at it! She also played the piano. It was fun to see her doing these things and having fun. I loved the days when our home was more harmonious. We had some days like that.

As we got older and moved out of the house, Dad related to us better as adults. He wasn't a "bounce us on his knee" kind of Dad. When my siblings were older, married, and had children, my parents loved seeing the grandchildren whenever they came back home.

Mom was a good cook. We'd have big Sunday dinners that brought my siblings home along with their spouses and children. The grandchildren were like a healing balm for my parents. Mom and Dad were on their best behavior when the grandchildren were coming. My parents were so peaceful and happy seeing the grandchildren. I couldn't wait to bring my own children into our home someday. Babies indeed bring joy; we all loved when they came over. We fussed over these sweet little ones. Whenever one of them cried or spilled something, anyone of us were happy to help them. We enjoyed all the baby hugs and kisses we could get. When my three older siblings married and began their families, I had just graduated from high school. My next move was to start school at a local college.

In September, I began attending Atlantic Community College, which opened up a whole new world of possibilities for my future. It was fall, my favorite season of the year. Being the first of my siblings to attend college, it was hard to know what to expect. It was a new challenge and a fresh new beginning.

Thankfully, several of my high school friends also attended Atlantic Community College. Our first two years of college gave us a taste of independence and the start of our grown-up life. College felt different from high school immediately. When moving from class to class and building to building on campus, the freedom we enjoyed was fun compared to staying in one building all day long. Driving a car to school rather than riding on a bus gave us time to socialize when we carpooled. There were so many ways we enjoyed our new unique school experience. In classes at ACC, we met new people, challenges, and opportunities. Our days were quite stimulating and diverse.

We had opportunities for growth and fun playing sports as well. Surprisingly, an invitation to join a team came from my gym teacher. ACC was starting a Varsity Girl's Tennis Team. For reasons unknown to me, Coach Abby invited me to join the team. At first, I declined her invitation.

"I've never played tennis before," I told Coach Abby.

"I know you'll be able to learn," she replied. After thinking it over, I joined the girl's tennis team.

Coach Abby convinced me she could teach me how to play tennis. As I learned how to play, I enjoyed the game. She assigned me to the position of number two singles player. Another girl and I were the only singles' players for our team, and the eight other girls were the teams' double players.

It was thrilling to be part of the very first ever Varsity Girl's Tennis Team for ACC. We did our best and learned all we could. Coach Abby assured us that success would come in time. We maintained a positive attitude and worked together well as a team. Our cooperation and willingness to help each other was outstanding. Coach Abby set a great example as she worked with each of us daily. She was an encourager and team builder.

Our first year was unsuccessful, which didn't surprise Coach Abby. It was our first year, and we got started a bit late in the season. One thing was for sure; we accomplished the start of a Varsity Girl's Tennis Team for ACC. Each of us was happy to do that; it was a privilege.

Being on the team gave me fond memories I enjoyed sharing with others for years to come. I'd tell about being the #2 girls' singles player on my college varsity tennis team. Intimidating as that may sound; initially I left out the lack of success part. Afterward, of course, I'd then tell the truth about our team and success (or lack of) that first year. It's always fun to share.

As team members, we had opportunities to make new friends at school and visit other campuses when we had away matches. It was excellent to stretch myself by participating in something new, and it was a good decision that I joined the team. Another wonderful thing happened during my first year of attending college.

Going to tennis practice and passing through the gym each day, I met a handsome young man named Bill. He was always there, lifting weights. It turns out he was practicing for weightlifting competitions, which he competed in locally.

Bill had big brown eyes, shiny brown hair, and a friendly smile. He was fit and friendly. We were talking one day, and he told me all about his lifting weights. It was his passion. Bill invited me to go to see one of his competitions. Never having attended a weightlifting competition before, I wasn't sure what to expect. Watching the heaviness of weights guys can lift was terrific. The feat looked impossible. Bill's working out and keeping fit all paid off, and he won many of his competitions. Within a few months, we started dating. Our relationship grew serious, and we became girlfriend and boyfriend.

We dated our whole first year. We attended dances, went to movies, out to dinner, bowling, and all kinds of things two young people do. By the end of that first year, Bill and I got engaged to be married. It would be a long-term engagement until we completed school. We both wanted to have a family one day. We were young freshman students, in love and naïve.

Attending Atlantic Community College gave me new beginnings in my college life and personal life. With these good things taking place, there was one personal issue for me to look into medically. I was 19 years old and had not menstruated. There were other signs of my maturing, so neither Mom nor I were concerned. Hair grew in all the right places, my breasts developed, and I even had monthly cramps, but no period. My oldest sister, Barbara, convinced Mom that I should see a doctor soon, and I did.

I made an appointment to see Dr. Brown, our family doctor. He ordered some scans and tests and referred me to a gynecological specialist in Philadelphia. Dr. Brown forwarded the test results up to the doctor there. Next, we made an appointment to see the specialist. Still not knowing what was wrong, Dr. Brown assured me the doctor he sent me to would know. Going to Philadelphia to see the specialist was a forty-minute drive from home, and Mom drove me to the appointment. I was happy she did.

Up until this point, Mom and I had never had a birds and bees discussion. My knowledge about female development was limited. Never having been to a gynecologist, it was a bit scary for me. Yet, I was hopeful that the specialist would tell me when my period would start.

We arrived at the doctor's office on time, and Mom parked in the parking garage. We entered the building and took an elevator to a top floor. As we entered the doctor's office, a friendly receptionist named Annie greeted us. She handed me a clipboard with some paperwork and asked me to fill out my information. After completing the form, I gave it back to Annie along with my insurance information. Shortly after, the doctor's assistant brought us into an exam room. Suddenly, feelings of nervousness came upon me. It was unsettling not knowing what was going to happen or what the doctor would say.

Mom and I sat quietly in the exam room. The silence was deafening, and yet I could hear my heartbeat thumping loudly. The nurse who took us into the room told me to take off my clothes, and she gave me a gown to put on. She instructed me to lie down, move to the edge with my knees up. Then she covered me with a sheet. Staring at the ceiling, I felt scared, vulnerable and anxious.

She said, "The doctor will be in shortly."

When the doctor came in, he introduced himself. He explained that he received my test results from Dr. Brown and he needed to examine me. Mom was in the room with me. So was the nurse. As the doctor examined me, I felt frightened. Part of it was painful. Never having had a gynecological exam, it was unsettling. He asked me several questions and then left the room. The nurse told me to get dressed, and she'd take us to the doctor's office. Once there, he would go over my test results and the physical exam he just completed.

Soon after, the nurse guided Mom and me down a long hallway leading to the doctor's office. I wondered why he couldn't talk with us in the same room he examined me. Going to his office seemed rather formal.

Upon entering, I immediately noticed the doctor had a serious look on his face, which gave me great concern. We sat across from him at his large, square, wooden desk. Peering down at my file, he reviewed my test results. His expression worried me. Within a few minutes, he gave us my devastating diagnosis, which changed my life forever! I could not wrap my young 19-year-old mind around the disastrous news he told us.

CONTEMPLATE & CONSIDER

❖ Do you remember when you did *not* get your period? Did you think you were just a late bloomer, like me? What were your concerns?

_____
_____
_____
_____
_____
_____
_____

❖ Use this space to write about your emotions on the day of your diagnosis. Tell your feelings, questions, and concerns.

_____
_____
_____
_____
_____
_____
_____

2

GRIPPED WITH GRIEF

This one day, this one doctor changed my life forever with his diagnosis. He closed the file and looked straight at me first and then at Mom.

He said to Mom, "Julie can never have children. She was born without a uterus. It's a rare condition that happens to one in five thousand women. It's called MRKH."

Shocked that he told Mom I would never have a child, I was in disbelief. Denial was my response. After all, I always planned to be a mom someday. *This news can't be true*, I thought.

He explained, "MRKH stands for the names of the doctors that named this condition; their names were: Mayer, Rokitansky, Küster, Hauser."

He continued telling us that this rare congenital disorder affects the female reproductive system. Women with MRKH are born without a womb or upper two-thirds of the birth canal. This genetic anomaly takes place during the mother's fetal development. When a woman cannot get her menstrual period in puberty, this is a sign of MRKH.

Hearing I had a rare condition and would never have children broke my heart. Tears fell from my eyes and flooded my lap.

I immediately grieved the children and family I would

never have and the hopes and dreams that have always been dear to my heart. None of them would ever happen. My young mind and spirit were in a state of shock.

I thought, *how could this be? There must be some mistake. Maybe we should get a second opinion.* My mind was racing, trying to grasp or understand this horrific news. Realizing I was different from every other woman and I couldn't be a mom was devastating.

Mom was silent and just listened to what the doctor was saying. No one even tried to console my broken heart. Tears flooded my body as I sobbed over this horrific news. Mom looked numb but continued to listen to the doctor's explanation of MRKH.

Believing a woman's purpose was to be a mom, my identity was shattered. I questioned my very existence.

I immediately thought, *God, why did you make me a woman that could NOT have children?* I was mad at God for the first time in my life. I believe He understood. Then I thought, *why go on in life? I have no purpose for being here.* Confused and upset that I couldn't conceive and give birth, I was more lost and alone than I've ever been.

For as long as I can remember, I always envisioned being a mom when I grew up. When I was a little girl, my favorite thing was to wheel my dolls in mom's baby carriage she used for us when we were infants and make-believe that I was a mom. I enjoyed pretending to be a mom and dreaming about the day I'd be one. Now, my dream was gone forever.

The doctor explained my options to have a family: by adoption or surrogacy. I was so young and filled with grief; I couldn't consider any of these at the moment. I was still trying to grasp this terrible truth about my body and its missing part.

Diagnosed in 1970, computers or cell phones did not exist yet; therefore, there was no way to reference my condition of MRKH. My body was unique and unlike all other women. I had questions about my body, with absolutely no answers. I wouldn't know any further information until 2012 (42 years later), when computers were available and in homes. From 1970 to 2012 was a long period of suffering in silence, with no support. After many years of silence, it wasn't even then that I could speak about it. My condition imprisoned me and took me hostage.

I could not Google "What is MRKH?" to find out more. There was no information anywhere about MRKH. I realized doctors didn't know what MRKH was. Every doctor's appointment, it was upsetting that they never heard of MRKH. I experienced great anxiety that the doctor did not know how my body differed from other women. I would think, what if something was wrong, and the doctor couldn't help me? Then what?

Learning of my MRKH was frightening and unsettling for me, physically and psychologically. I thought I'd go through my entire life and never meet another person in the world with MRKH. I can't remember if the doctor brought up counseling. I didn't have any counseling, which surely would've helped to sort out my feelings.

Today, when a woman is diagnosed with MRKH, counseling is immediately recommended. It is best to have counseling to process MRKH. There are trained people to help women grasp and understand their MRKH. I was alone, with no support.

On the ride home from our appointment in Philadelphia, Mom was silent. She may have been concerned my MRKH was her fault. We know today, MRKH has no cause. Our drive home was long, and I sobbed rivers of silent tears. It could have been helpful if Mom would have talked with me about my diagnosis, but she didn't. I needed her help to process my bad news. In my shyness, I was silent and did not speak with her about it either.

When we reached home and approached the house, my younger brothers, Bobby and Joey, were outside playing and saw us pull up to the front of our home. They ran to the car and asked us how we did at our doctor's appointment.

Mom blurted out, "Julie's OK; she can't have kids." When I heard her response, it took my breath away.

My brothers replied, "Oh," and ran off to play again. I felt worse when Mom told my brothers the way she did. I thought, was Mom that aloof about my diagnosis? It couldn't be, for it was earth-shattering for me. I was NOT OK. Getting out of the car; I ran into the house, up the stairs, slammed my bedroom door shut, and cried myself to sleep.

In hindsight, it was good that Mom took me to the doctors, for I'd never have been able to hear that news and be able to drive home. Grief overwhelmed me. After this day, my family never mentioned my MRKH again. We dealt with it by pretending I never had the diagnosis. It was rare and unnoticeable. It was as though we swept it under the rug. Unfortunately for me, it consumed my daily life. I was grieving my own life but was still alive. Devastation filled my soul. I had no way to envision my future.

My MRKH was impossible to share with anyone; it was private. I couldn't even tell my closest girlfriend. There was one person, I'd have to tell, my fiancé Bill. I felt I should explain it to him, so I did. Telling Bill about my MRKH didn't go well. We broke up. Now there was even more grief for me. My life felt like it was over.

Then, not only was I sad about not being able to have children, I thought to myself, who would want to marry me if I couldn't have children? Would I ever find a man who could live with this condition I had? What kind of future could I possibly have? Maybe I'd never get married. Such uncertainty, confusion, and sorrow to bear at a young age were difficult. Regardless, life had to go on.

What is odd for women with MRKH is that we look completely normal on the outside. No one knows how different we are. With MRKH, there can also be other anomalies. The anomalies can differ from one woman with MRKH to another. It would be years later, when we had computers, I learned much more. On the day of my diagnosis, we only spoke about my not being able to have children of my own. For decades after the diagnosis, my life was one of isolation, confusion, despair, and unanswered questions.

I took one day at a time. It wasn't easy. I just focused on my classes and continued to play on the tennis team. It was harder to concentrate now, yet I was determined to complete school. Inside of me was this horrible secret that I had MRKH. My body was different from every other girl's on campus. The psychological impact of this diagnosis gave me a lifetime of lament.

Coping with my MRKH was how I handled my parent's alcoholism, facing each day as if everything was fine. It wasn't. We kept our parent's alcoholism a secret, and now my MRKH was a secret. I became quite a good secret-keeper. Putting on a mask of normalcy, pretending that everything was fine, is how I dealt with it. No one could guess the amount of sadness inside of me. Had counseling been available, it would have helped me feel, heal and grieve.

For women with MRKH, there are many triggers to our sadness everywhere. In my family, my cute nieces and nephews caused me to have two opposite emotions in my heart at the same time: joy for my niece or nephew and for my siblings as parents and sadness for me. Of course, I had joy loving on them; yet they reminded me of what I could not have, my own children.

The year I was diagnosed, I had two nieces and a nephew. Soon after, there were two more nieces and a nephew. Seeing my sisters and sister-in-law pregnant gave me great sorrow because I knew I would never be able to experience carrying a child. It seemed motherhood would not happen for me. I would not be a mom, or so I thought. The triggers to my sorrow were always, often, and forever.

MRKH is not something you get over, like a cold or flu. It is a condition that, over time, you learn to accept. Not speaking about MRKH with my family intensified my heartache. They were completely unaware of my sorrow. Eventually, I realized that my silence all those years was taken by my family as total acceptance and being "over it" myself. I was amazed they could think I was OK with my childlessness.

Watching siblings, friends, and even strangers, having babies, husbands, and a family life broke my heart. Going to baby showers was almost impossible. Children's birthday parties were hard. With all my nieces and nephews, there were parties for them each and every year. The reminders kept coming, and my grief was unending and accumulating. Being happy for the birthday boy or girl, I hid my heartache. Birthday parties were normal, but I was not.

Crying out to God turned out to be my saving grace, literally. I believed He heard and knew the anguish of my soul. I sensed His presence. I thought He knew exactly how I felt. He would be the only one to carry me through my extreme sadness. Without God, I was utterly alone in my sorrow. He was there for me. I just knew He was.

If not for His presence, I don't know how I would have survived my childlessness. He helped me through my darkness day by day. I wondered if God had a reason for allowing me to be born with MRKH. He must have had a specific plan; it was all I believed: I just didn't know His plan yet.

My first two years of college were great joy. It all took a turn for the worst when I learned of my diagnosis of MRKH. Bill and I broke up, and my entire world changed forever. Those years at ACC were like a roller coaster ride with the greatest joys and deepest sorrows within these two years of my young life. Graduating from ACC and moving away from home to complete my college education offered me joy in the midst of suffering.

Julie around the age she was diagnosed with MRKH.

CONTEMPLATE & CONSIDER

❖ When you were diagnosed, were you offered counseling? If so, did you receive it? Write your thoughts…

_____
_____
_____
_____
_____
_____
_____

❖ Having a diagnosis of MRKH, grieving is a necessary response. Have you grieved? To "heal" we need to "feel". Allow your feelings to be expressed and not suppressed.

_____
_____
_____
_____
_____
_____
_____

3

JOY IN THE MIDST
OF SUFFERING

The following two years at Glassboro State College (now called Rowan) were brand new experiences living away from home with my roommates. Moving out of my house and into a shared apartment was exciting. Although still suffering silently, these years at Glassboro proved to be a breath of fresh air and brought peace and joy back into my life.

The MRKH Syndrome was unknown to my new roommates, and it was as though I left it under the rug at home. MRKH was always with me, but I did my best not to focus on it or share it with others. The distraction of a new way of life, being on a new campus, and setting up our home away from home was positive for my mental health. It was also tons of fun for all of us girls.

My roommates were Tina, Rosemary, and Annie. Tina and Rosemary were friends I already knew from Holy Spirit High School. Annie, I met at Atlantic Community College. We all graduated from Atlantic Community College at the same time. We were excited to venture out on our own and rent an apartment together that was within five miles of our new school.

Gathering all of our resources, belongings, and furniture together, our new apartment became "home." Decorating it with whatever we could find was fun. Tina and I shared one bedroom. We purchased colorful curtains for our bedroom, and they brightened up the room. The curtains gave our room a well-decorated look. Each of the bedrooms had two single beds. Tina and I arranged our beds the long way against the walls, so they looked like sofas and made our room look bigger.

One of the girls got an overstuffed, comfy, light green couch and matching chair for our living room. It was perfect. The couch was the most significant piece of furniture we had. We also had a TV and stand on the opposite wall. All of us put our money together to buy a small dinette set. We had the perfect spot for our table and chairs, just outside our kitchen area by a half wall alongside the kitchen. The dinette set was cute and functional. We had many great times around that little table eating, studying, and simply talking.

Our apartment's location was about an hour from where our parents lived and just a few minutes to campus. We felt so grown up, being on our own, it was a first for all of us.

My roommates and I got along exceptionally well. Thankfully, my depression lifted. We launched into what became two years of great times, happy memories, deepened friendships, and completion of our education. As mentioned previously, my roomies didn't know about my MRKH. For now, it was still my secret.

Having dinner together each night, we laughed, recalling the events of our day. We were like a family. We focused on our classes and had fun every day. Our stories became a treasure of memories we would enjoy for years to come. Our crazy college days were unforgettable.

During our first semester at Glassboro, Rosemary and I had mostly activity courses for our major. Physical Education courses like swimming, field hockey, rhythms and dance were part of our first semester. The activity of our classes left us physically exhausted. Our bodies became muscular from the amount of exercise we were getting. Questioning if I was in the right major, I considered changing it, but had not mentioned that to Rosemary yet.

Tina and Annie, in their elementary education program, had stories as well. Yet, they were both happy with their curriculum. Rosemary's and my stories kept us all laughing around our dinner table.

One of our favorite stories was Rosemary's and my Field Hockey Class and our first practice game. One early frigid September morning, when the teacher wanted us to demonstrate what we learned days earlier, it was a concern for me because I still did not understand the game. I truly dreaded this practice game we were about to play. I told Rosemary, "I'm in big trouble; I still don't understand the different positions and what part of the field we are supposed to cover."

Rosemary and I were exhausted that morning, having stayed up late the night before. The temperature was in the 30's and turned our fingers purple. They felt frozen. Our cheeks were red, and we could see our breath in the air. The weather felt more like January. Our ugly dark green sweat suits (uniform for this class) were not keeping us very warm. Our teacher was soon to find out about my not knowing how to play this game. She assigned me the wing position, and we all went out on the field to play.

As our class began playing in our first ever practice game, within seconds, the Coach yelled out to me in a loud, angry voice, "Rosasco, (that was my maiden name) you're a wing!"

Clueless, I yelled to my roommate, who was in the middle of the field, "Rosemary, what's a wing?" Rosemary laughed so hard she couldn't respond.

Not to anyone's surprise, I didn't do well in field hockey. My teacher realized I did not understand how to play this game, and sadly, I had no desire to learn either. Years later, when we recall that story, we laugh so hard that we cry.

Funny stories and all, it was still a question if physical education was the right major for me. After meeting with my counselor, we changed my major to Elementary Education. Fortunately, switching to the new curriculum, it was still possible to graduate with my roommates on time.

Happy the change in majors worked out; elementary education was a better fit for me. As an elementary education major, we had a program called a practicum experience. We were assigned to a local elementary school to observe in an actual classroom. It was exciting to be with a real classroom and teacher and to be with them for several weeks. Being assigned to Ms. Pat Smith's third-grade classroom, I gradually taught one reading group or some other lesson to the students. We progressed by taking on teaching a little more each day. We actively taught in this class over several weeks and kept adding one more subject until we taught for an entire day. It was an exciting and challenging assignment.

Ms. Pat Smith was an excellent third-grade teacher and an outstanding leader for me to follow. She taught me so much. I hoped I could be as good a teacher as her someday.

The third-grade children were a joy to be around. These days were fun because the children loved giving us (their teachers) love notes and drawings. The kids were adorable, and we bonded nicely. I had such love for these sweet children. Yet, I realized I'd never have my own 3rd grader.

Teaching a lesson each day and adding to them daily, my entire day to teach finally came. I felt ready for it, but nervous. At the end of my first full day of teaching, I was grateful to have made it through with lots of happy memories. This Practicum experience was a real-life experience of what it felt like to be a teacher. That night, I couldn't wait to share my first full day with my roommates.

Besides school life and our fun and crazy dinner stories, my roomies and I had a social life. We attended dances, parties, and things like that. Sometimes we entertained ourselves with movies. Once in a while, we made up funny choreographed dances in our apartment. We had friends over occasionally and always got along well with each other for these two years.

My sister Mare was married and lived within a few minutes of our apartment. Her husband, Dave worked out of town often. Mare and Dave had their first child, Davey. He was an infant at the time my roomies and I lived near them. We enjoyed going over to their house to see my sister and little Davey. He was so cute with his chubby little cheeks.

On one visit, I remember Davey was sick with a terrible cold. His tiny nose was crusty and bleeding a bit. I took a damp, soft tissue and got him all cleaned up. I held him for a while until he fell asleep in my arms. Shortly after, Mare took him and put him in his crib. It was a special mommy moment to hold my nephew, Davey, and snuggle him until he fell asleep. I cherished this time with him. I always loved seeing Davey and all my nieces and nephews, yet it was a bittersweet experience because of my MRKH.

Once in a while, my roommates and I went to parties at

friends' apartments. At parties is where I first drank alcohol. Alcohol was not good in my system, it made me depressed. All my sadness with MRKH, the recent break-up with Bill, all surfaced. My heart was still broken. We never drank in our own apartment, only when we went to a party. One day I finally told my roommates about my MRKH. They said how sad they were for me. Like at home, we never spoke about it again. I believe they understood my sadness.

Sharing my MRKH news with Tina, Rosemary, and Annie was a healthy thing to do. It took the pressure off of me keeping my secret. I wanted to be authentic with them. Then when I was sad, they understood. Triggers to my MRKH were often and everywhere.

In between our junior and senior year of school, we went on a winter break to Florida. It was a 22 + hr. drive. What fun! We packed up lots of food to eat on the way to save time and money and took turns driving. Vacationing with friends and going to Florida were firsts for me.

Florida welcomed us with bright sunshine, warm balmy weather, swaying beautiful palm trees, pretty flowers in bloom, and lots of green grass. The air smelled refreshing, as we could smell the flowers and trees. Florida was beautiful. The weather, warm and sunny, was different from New Jersey, where it was winter. It was perfect pool weather. We loved it. Feeling like we were in paradise, we made the most of the enjoyable warm sunny days and left with good tans.

Our hotel room provided a place to cook in the room. Watching our budget, we cooked most of our meals there. We were as thrifty as we could be. One day we did one of our choreographed dance routines in the lobby of this little hotel. We did a simple tap dance. I don't know why we did it. You do lots of funny things when you're young. The people loved our dance, and we got a hearty round of applause. They probably thought, *what crazy kids*. Our vacation ended, and we took our long drive back home.

Before we knew it, our two years at Glassboro were over. After graduation, we packed up all our things and moved back home. Other than a few years later, for weddings, I didn't see my roommates often at first. We lost touch during our childbearing years and reunited years later. When we reunited, it was as though we had never been apart. We share a special bond for which I am forever grateful. Tina, Rosemary, Annie, and I were and still are a family unit.

With college complete, my priority was to search for a teaching job. A school nearby was advertising for an elementary school teacher, so I stopped by and gave them my resume. When I did, they were kind enough to schedule an appointment for me to interview with them that week.

The interview, although grueling, with five people interviewing me at once, went well. After the interview, they told me there were a few more candidates to see and that they would get back to me. Grateful for the opportunity to meet with them, I expressed my thanks and waited to hear from them.

Two weeks later, a letter from the superintendent's office arrived at my house. Saying a brief prayer as I opened my letter, I was thrilled to read that I got the job to teach third grade at New York Avenue School. Oh my, I'd have my very own third-grade class! I was happy to have gotten a teaching job after college.

I quickly told Mom and Dad, and they were happy for me. Although they had difficulties with each other, they were very supportive of me completing my college education. I hoped Mom and Dad were proud that I graduated from college and landed a teaching job too.

Looking back at the number of times God was good to me, He always had my back. His love was there, even when I was unaware of it. I still wondered what His plan was. For now, teaching a classroom full of children in September, was the immediate plan. It was exciting anticipating meeting and teaching my students.

In August, teachers went into school to set up their classrooms, and so did I. Starting with great anticipation, it was nice meeting all my fellow teachers who were getting their classrooms ready. Everyone welcomed me, knowing I was new. Many of them offered to give me whatever help I needed. I felt at home and welcome in my new environment right away because of their kindness.

Preparing my classroom, I wanted to make it inviting and interesting for the children as they entered their school on the first day. Putting up our flag, decorating all the bulletin boards as attractively as I could, and preparing as much as possible was exciting. Consumed with joy and nervousness, I looked forward to September.

Also, moving back home after living away was difficult. I missed living with friends and enjoying my independence. However, being home for a while, granted me the time to find a summer job and to look for a place to rent with a friend.

CONTEMPLATE & CONSIDER

❖ Have you considered getting a job working with children?

_____
_____
_____
_____
_____
_____
_____

❖ Are you able to focus on school or a job, and does that give you relief from feelings?

_____
_____
_____
_____
_____
_____
_____

Julie with her roommates, years
later, Rosemary, Tina & Annie.

4

DATE WITH DESTINY

Knowing I was seeking employment until I started my teaching job in the fall, Dad arranged for me to meet a fine restaurant owner in Longport, New Jersey, a town nearby. Mr. and Mrs. Flynn, the owners of the Longport Inn, were Dad's clients. After interviewing with them, they hired me as a waitress for the summer. Dad had a knack of referring people to each other with his gifted personality. I was grateful for his help and excited to get the job.

The Longport Inn was a fantastic place to work. The servers earned great tips. I quickly learned to serve well to make the income to live on my own again. Here the customers were pleasant, the food was excellent, and this job became a doorway to my future. It was a blessing to me in more ways than I could have imagined.

While working, I mentioned to my co-workers that I needed to rent an apartment soon and find a roommate. Barbara, one server about my age, said she was looking for an apartment and roommate as well. Barbara taught elementary school in another school district. She was a blast to work with, and we got along very well. We had a lot in common, so we looked for a place to rent together. Barbara and I found a rental, and I was fortunate to find another nice roommate in her.

We rented a second-floor furnished apartment in Ocean City. This town is a popular family vacation area, complete with a boardwalk and beach. The place we rented was within a few minutes of the beach and only about ten minutes from my family. I was happy to live close by but on my own. I enjoyed my independence. Our apartment was only 15 minutes from where we worked as waitresses and close to our teaching jobs. Our rental home had everything we needed. The landlords were a friendly family that lived on the first floor.

Our apartment's entrance was up an outside wooden stairway to a large deck on the second floor. This outdoor area was great for cooking or stargazing at night. Entering the large kitchen with a turquoise painted wooden table and four chairs was inviting. The table and chairs looked pretty as they accented the dark maroon vinyl flooring well. Straight ahead was the living room with a large picture window from which we could see the entire neighborhood. To the left of the living room was a hallway with a bathroom. The hallway led to two bedrooms, one to the left and one to the right. The floor plan was perfect for Barbara and me.

Our new home, fully furnished, had everything from furniture to dishes, bowls, glasses, and silverware. Our apartment fit all the criteria we needed. As we settled into our new place, Barbara and I were excited to see what the summer in Ocean City would bring.

That summer, we were swamped working in the restaurant and looking forward to teaching in the fall. I learned Barbara had an identical twin sister named Nancy. I met Nancy one day, and they looked identical. Both were pretty girls. Nancy was married, lived nearby, and worked in radio advertising. While doing her job one day, she visited a new nightclub in Somers Point, called Admiral Al's.

Nancy thought they might want to buy advertising to get the word out for their new business. She was right. The owner Alan purchased advertising from Nancy's company.

While there, Nancy met a bartender named Ted, who immediately took a liking to her. She quickly told Ted she was married but had an identical twin sister named Barbara, and Barbara was single.

Nancy asked Ted, "Would you like to meet Barbara?"

Ted replied, "Yes, I sure would."

Nancy had Ted and Barbara meet. They liked each other right away. Within a few weeks of moving into our new apartment, Barbara was dating Ted, and they became very close. I wondered what might happen next.

Barbara immediately wanted me to meet her new boyfriend, Ted, and also his roommate, Terry. I wasn't quite ready to meet someone. Barbara did not know about my MRKH or my breakup with Bill. It was nice of her to want to introduce me to Terry. I met her boyfriend Ted, and I liked him. Barbara and Ted were a cute couple.

Ted, who lived up in north Jersey, worked at Admiral Al's just for the summer. He rented in a town nearby called Margate. Ted's roommate, Terry, also worked at Admiral Al's as a bartender. Terry was from North Jersey as well. Since Ted and Terry were roommates in Margate, Barbara came up with the idea of roommates dating roommates. Barbara knew that Terry, Ted's roommate, was single.

Barbara was relentless in trying to convince me to go on a double date to meet Terry. I resisted for quite some time, telling her I didn't feel ready.

Weeks later, Terry and I met. Instead of a date where the guys came and picked us up, Barbara and I met them where they worked at Admiral Al's. Although they were both bartenders, they weren't working the night we met them. It was less formal meeting Ted and Terry at Admiral Al's.

Before going to Admiral Al's with Barbara to meet the guys, it was stressful thinking about what to wear to meet Terry. It was the shore and very casual. Something nice, comfortable and attractive is what I settled on wearing. It was time to meet the guys.

The night Terry and I met was unforgettable and humorous. After stressing out over what to wear to meet him, his outfit almost sent me running out the door, seriously. Meeting Terry, I glanced at him and thought, what is going on with this guy and his outfit? Terry had on cut-off jean shorts, flip-flops, and worst of all, a cut-off tee shirt. Yes, a cut-off tee shirt. His belly was showing. Oh my! Terry took this casual shore thing to a whole other level. Seeing him dressed this way, I considered running out the door but didn't. I wasn't sure what to do. After we talked a little and got to know each other, turning and running wasn't necessary.

More shocking than his outfit were the first words he said after he and I were introduced. Looking straight into my eyes, with a smile on his face, he said, "I think I'm in love."

How do I respond to that? I thought. I didn't. I just stood there and smiled back at him.

He asked me what I wanted to drink, and I told him. Off he went to the bar and came back with our drinks. When Terry went to get our drinks, it gave me time to process all that just happened and talk to my roommate, Barbara.

"I don't know about this guy, Barbara. What's with his outfit?" I questioned. Barbara smiled and giggled.

I stayed a while and got to know Terry a little better. We talked, danced, and enjoyed getting to know each other and had a good time after all. Once I got past the outfit and the first words Terry spoke to me, he seemed to be a pretty nice guy. He was intelligent, and I liked that about him. He had a great sense of humor, which I also found attractive. We both enjoyed dancing, and we danced a lot. We had a fun night together.

As a former hippy, Terry had long blonde hair. He had beautiful blue eyes, a mustache, and a great smile. Terry was eight years older than me. This first date turned out to be very interesting. Seeing Terry, his outfit, and thinking about his first words to me reminded me of the old saying, "Never judge a book by its cover." Had I left Admiral Al's that night because of his outfit or strange first words right away, my life would have turned out differently.

We went out again and began seeing more of each other. It was amazing to me that Terry was indeed an extraordinary individual. He kept my curiosity piqued, wanting to know more about him. His confident personality was unlike anyone I'd ever met. There was never a loss for words with our conversation, and I liked that. It's so hard if a conversation doesn't flow, especially on a first date.

Over time, Terry shared his travel stories with me. He had traveled extensively in his lifetime, and I loved hearing about his adventures. He captivated me with his willingness to share the stories of his unique and adventurous lifestyle.

After meeting that first night, Terry's outfits were much better on future dates. I was attracted to his individuality. In the back of my mind, I wondered how he would handle knowing about my MRKH. However, I did not tell him about it for quite some time.

Barbara was happy to see her matchmaking resulted in roommates dating roommates after all. Terry and I continued to date that entire summer. So did Barbara and Ted. September came and Barbara and I started teaching, and Terry and Ted went back up north to their jobs. Our adventurous summer ended.

Terry's full-time career was teaching high school History in North Jersey. Besides teaching, Terry, was President of the Teacher's Association and handled the school district's negotiations. The jobs that went along with that were teacher grievances, disputes, and things like that. He was a coach and on weekends a bartender; he was quite the worker.

When fall came, Terry went back north to teach and bartend weekends but would pass up weekend work every so often to visit me in Ocean City. I was glad to see him as we dated the entire summer. I never told Terry about my MRKH. I don't think I ever told my roommate Barbara either.

One weekend, while Terry visited, I wanted him to meet my parents. We had a date to go out to dinner. Terry agreed to meet Mom and Dad at their home before we went out that night. I requested he get his hair cut before meeting my parents. Not sure how Terry would react; I just knew my parents would not like to see Terry with long hair. Amazingly, Terry got his hair cut.

The night Terry showed up at my parent's home, he shocked me. His appearance compared to when I first met him was the total opposite. With his hair cut, mustache trimmed, and dressed in a beautiful blue leisure suit with shoes (not flip-flops), he looked very handsome. His blue suit brought out his sparkling blue eyes. I had never seen him dressed so well.

We had an enjoyable visit with my parents. Terry is a great conversationalist, and so was my Dad on many topics. They all took a liking to each other right away. I was happy the introduction went so well. Our visit with Mom and Dad was just the beginning of an unforgettable night.

We left my parent's home and went to a popular seafood restaurant in Somers Point. The server came by and gave us menus and took our drink order. On this night, I planned to tell Terry about my MRKH syndrome. I was extremely nervous. While waiting for our food, we talked a bit about our visit with Mom and Dad. Terry was happy to meet them and said he enjoyed speaking with them. I could tell by our visit, they liked him a lot too.

As we talked, my mind went blank about how to tell Terry about my MRKH, but I just knew it was time to tell him. I started with, "Terry, I have something to tell you."

"Okay, what's that?" he asked.

I told him, "In 1970 I had a diagnosis of MRKH, which is rare and happens to 1 in 5000 women. I was born without a uterus and cannot have children of my own."

Terry's reaction floored me. He had a huge grin on his face that went from ear to ear. I thought, what's that grin all about? I never imagined Terry would respond like that!

"What are you smiling about?" I asked.

"I have two beautiful daughters, six and seven years old," he replied.

"Really?" I responded, as shock and hope filled my spirit. He explained that he and the girls lived with his parents since

43

the girls were infants.

"Their names are Lori and Kim. They both have red hair and freckles. They look like you." Terry said.

Wow! I thought.

Terry went on to explain that he was married at a young age, and was now divorced for several years. Of course, I wanted to hear everything about the girls. Our conversation went right through dinner, dessert, and beyond—what a fantastic night.

Terry came over to my place, and we talked for hours and hours. I had zillions of questions for him. There were no cell phones, so he couldn't pull out his phone and show me pictures or anything. Terry's news of having children and his reaction to my MRKH was very positive. Thank God. It appeared my news of having MRKH would not end our relationship. This entire night was memorable from start to finish.

Our meeting felt like a date with destiny. We enjoyed each other. Terry had children, and I couldn't have children. His having two daughters was exciting news for me to know. My MRKH was not a problem for him. This night will always be a beautiful memory of how good God is.

If Terry and I ever married, I'd be a stepmom. Terry was so happy to tell me all about his beautiful girls, Lori and Kim. The atmosphere that entire night was one of surprise, joy and discovery.

Terry explained he moved back to his parent's home so they could help raise the girls. They were infants, and Rose and Ed were thrilled to have them move in. Lori and Kim became the daughters Rose always wanted. Rose had two boys, Ed and Terry. She asked the girls to call her Mom, and they did, even though she was their grandma. They called their biological mother, Mom too. Barbara, their Mom, lived nearby. Terry commuted forty-five miles each way daily to live at his parent's house with the girls and work as a teacher in Ewing.

I remember meeting the girls several weeks later when I drove up to Terry's parent's home. The girls knew I was coming up to meet them. When I pulled up to Rose and Ed's house, these adorable red-headed, freckle-faced, smiling, giggling girls were at the front door, which was halfway open. They were trying to get a glimpse of me.

The moment I laid eyes on the girls, I loved them. They captured my heart, and we gave each other a big group hug. The girls were adorable, and we talked and got to know each other a bit that day. Meeting Lori and Kim was a beautiful experience and made me happy.

I also met Terry's parents. Ed, Terry's dad, came out to meet me first, but he wasn't so crazy about me. He was an immigrant from Ireland and asked me about my Italian last name. He let me know right away that he didn't care for Italian people.

"Well, my mom is Irish. Surely you could like half of me, right?" I said with a smile on my face. Telling Ed about liking the Irish half of me was my humorous attempt to diffuse his profound statement about not liking Italian people. He looked confused, not sure yet. I didn't let Ed's attitude wreck my day meeting Lori and Kim.

Rose, Terry's mom, was quiet and shy. She said little, but she had a beautiful smile and a twinkle in her eyes. Just like

Terry, when Rose smiled, her smile went from ear to ear. I thought maybe I was a threat to her. It was unusual for Terry to bring someone home to meet Rose, Ed, and the girls. She may have been worried that if we married, she'd lose the girls. Rose was quiet, observant, and lovely. We got along fine. Neither of them knew about my MRKH.

Meeting Lori and Kim filled my heart with love, joy, and a desire to know them better. I looked forward to seeing what the future might have in store for us. Rose and Ed were happy to meet me, even with Ed's initial complaint about my being half Italian. In time, Ed learned to accept me, and we grew very fond of each other.

The following day, I called my parents about my exciting news about Terry having two daughters. Knowing I couldn't have my own children, Mom and Dad were happy for me. Our date did feel like a date with destiny!

CONTEMPLATE & CONSIDER

❖ Has MRKH been a problem with a relationship you have had or are having?

_____
_____
_____
_____
_____
_____
_____

❖ A break-up resulting from MRKH is protection for you. That person is not the right person. Trust there is someone better. What do you think?

_____
_____
_____
_____
_____
_____

"You are not an accident. You are one of a kind. You're big dream is from God, and it's irreplaceable. And you were born to seize it and celebrate it every day of your life!"

— Bruce Wilkinson

5

MARRIED WITH CHILDREN

One year later, the roommates dating roommates resulted in Barbara and Ted getting married. Terry and I married at the end of my second year of teaching in Somers Point. June through August became busy months for us.

Our wedding was planned for August, we had a lot to do. I needed to secure a teaching position where we'd be living after we married. We also had to find an apartment to rent. With finalizing our wedding plans, this was an extremely hectic time.

It was 1975, just five years after my MRKH diagnosis, and wondering if I'd ever get married. Thus, becoming married with children was more than I could have imagined. Our life together was about to begin.

Fortunately, the same school system Terry taught in, Ewing Township, hired me. In September, I'd be teaching third-grade. It was my third year of teaching third grade. God is good.

Terry and I found an affordable two-story duplex to rent in a town called West Trenton. It was across from a beautiful park. It would be perfect for Terry, me, and the girls. Initially, Terry told me about the possibility of the girls staying with Rose and Ed. Regardless, I remained hopeful that Lori and Kim would come and live with us.

Our wedding plans took shape with lots of help from my sister, Barbara, and her husband, Joe. What an exciting time!

Since Terry's and my family lived two hours away from each other, we held our wedding geographically mid-way for everyone's convenience. We got married in Neptune, a town that was an hour trip for both families. Neptune was a location that my family and I were familiar with because we used to live there.

My older siblings, their spouses, and my grandparents still lived in Neptune. Dad, Mom, and the rest of us moved away from Neptune to South Jersey because of Dad's job transfer. South Jersey, or the "Jersey shore," as it is referred to, was where I met Terry the summer before.

My sister, Barbara, and her husband, Joe, lived in Neptune and offered to help us with our wedding day. We are forever grateful for them making this day so special. Barbara and Joe held the before and after party for us at their beautiful home. It was lovely and open to our wedding guests and family. Barbara and Joe are gracious hosts. They always make everyone feel welcome in their home.

Gathering everyone at their home was a huge help since the wedding was being held in Neptune. Our photographer's pictures, with the backdrop of their home and gardens, are precious memories of our wedding day we look back on and enjoy.

Our wedding party consisted of my two sisters Barbara and Mary Jane; in their country-style dresses with a tiny, delicate blue rose print, with off-white lace trim. They wore blue, wide

rim, straw bonnets. The guys, Joe, Ed, and Terry, had light tan tuxes with brown velvet piping and off-white ruffle shirts. Everyone looked stunning.

As our official driver, my younger brother Bobby, 20 years old, drove Barbara and Joe's 1966 dark green Lincoln Continental with its blacktop. It looked just like a limo. Bobby was thrilled to be our chauffeur and drive this cool limo-like car. He did an outstanding job. It was a fond memory for Bobby and us. He talked about his role in our wedding for years.

My gown, a full-length, light beige dress with embroidered lace down the front, back, and sleeves, was pretty, simple, and reasonably priced. The dress was just right for me: not too fancy, but elegant and unique. I bought a veil at a local bridal salon. It matched the dress perfectly and made the dress look like it, too, was from the bridal salon. The veil trailed down past my dress and had an embroidered edge and mesh, matching my dress in color and design. Both were a great find.

The church we married in was Our Lady of Mount Carmel Catholic Church. When we lived in Neptune, this was my family's church, and it was gorgeous inside and out. The pictures of the marriage ceremony were stunning with the painted arched ceiling on the altar of the church.

The wedding went on as scheduled on August 23, 1975, when Terry and I said our "I do's" and became Mr. and Mrs. Coveney. After the wedding, everyone went to the reception held at the Jumping Brook Country Club.

Our wedding day was magical. Having everyone we loved in one place to celebrate with us was beyond what any words could describe. My stepdaughters, Lori and Kim, looked pretty in their matching long dresses.

During the wedding, Kim slipped away and changed into her first Holy Communion dress to surprise us. Taking hold of my bridal bouquet, she posed in one of our pictures. She looked like a little bride, and she expressed her individuality that day in the most adorable way.

I enjoyed seeing our girls, their cousins and other children having fun together. Watching conversations around the room, I was curious if people were talking about who the girls would live with. Glancing over at Terry's mom, I reflected on what she was thinking, but there was no way to know.

All the adults were enjoying themselves. There was lots of dancing, laughter and getting to know one another. I enjoyed meeting my new family and seeing my relatives I hadn't seen in a long time. It was nearly impossible for me to sit down and eat. I wanted to visit everyone.

The celebration for our wedding continued afterwards at Barbara and Joe's home. No one wanted to leave, including us. We were all having a great time and didn't want it to end. Once we left, Terry and I headed to Portland, Maine, for our honeymoon.

I was married, had children, a new home, teaching job. Sadly, I learned that day, Lori and Kim would stay with Rose and Ed initially. The plan was to give us time as newlyweds to settle into our new life. It also kept the girls in their same schools, neighborhood, and the environment they had been in since infancy. It was not determined how long they would stay with their grandparents. In the beginning, the idea of the girls living with Terry's parents seemed good for the girls, and I'm sure Rose and Ed were thrilled too. It gave Terry and me time to adjust to our new life together. It all made sense to me at first.

When we could, we soaked up our time with Lori and Kim as much as possible. Visiting them on weekends, we always had a great time. We especially enjoyed our summer or extended school holidays when we could take the girls on vacations. Since we both taught school, we had the same holidays as the girls and we all had summers off.

Lots of our friends from school had young children, and I wished we had our girls or had a little one that we could've adopted. My desire to be a mom was more significant now than ever before, being 24 years old, married and in my child-bearing years. My new friends didn't know about my MRKH. Being with friends and their children, it would have been nice for our girls to be with us and have fun with our friend's kids too. My sadness heightened. I was missing my girls.

The subject of us starting our own family always came up. Quickly, we talked about our two beautiful daughters. Terry's friends knew about Lori and Kim, but I think they still wondered if we'd also have more children. I always gave vague answers to put their questions off. These inquiries about us having kids of our own were heartaches because I longed to have children.

Considering counseling, I wondered, where would I even begin to share my story? Most likely, counselors, like doctors, wouldn't have heard of MRKH either. Thinking back on this now, I'm sure counseling could have helped me. It felt uncomfortable that MRKH was rare. I wasn't able to talk about it. My secretiveness intensified my brokenness psychologically. I once heard the expression: "You're only as sick as your secrets." If true, I was pretty sick. Grieving alone, feelings of lament continued daily, monthly, and yearly.

Terry and I talked about my MRKH, but he couldn't fully understand on an emotional level what this was like for me as a woman. The triggers that would increase my emotional turmoil were everywhere, I couldn't escape them.

I questioned God again and talk to Him frequently, believing and sensing He listens each time I speak to Him. God was and is still my lifeline. He is my Counselor. Unlike my anger with Him when I was first diagnosed, my communication with Him turned into a search for: "why God?" Still no answers, but I felt comfort knowing He heard me. I believed He would reveal His plan for me one day.

Terry and I talked about adopting. He shared how his first child, Shawn, passed away while he was still an infant. He would have been Lori and Kim's older brother. Shawn's death was very difficult for both Terry and his first wife. I understood. Terry's loss of his son played into his decision of not wanting to adopt an infant.

Terry was happy with our two beautiful girls. I was too, but I yearned to raise them and have a baby as well. With Terry's experience of his son dying, I would not push my desire to have a child. I accepted the fact that we would not adopt. To make matters worse, the girls' situation at their grandparent's home didn't change quickly either. Therefore, I had children but didn't have them.

Not being able to make sense of anything relating to motherhood, I thought perhaps God had a whole other plan. Believing He did, gave me a ray of hope. I did my best to remain positive, and was attentive to see if I could recognize what God was showing me. This coincided nicely with my search for my identity five years later, in 1980.

"Oftentimes, the more we surrender to God, the greater our ability to see His hand in our life."

— Charles Stanley

CONTEMPLATE & CONSIDER

❖ Have you experienced disappointment about an
   expected event in your life?

_____

_____

_____

_____

_____

_____

_____

❖ Is motherhood a desire? Is so, what ways have you
   considered to become a mother?

_____

_____

_____

_____

_____

_____

_____

6

SEARCHING FOR MY IDENTITY

In 1980 Terry was selling real estate part-time, on nights and weekends, in addition to his teaching. It was interesting for me to listen to Terry on the phone with his clients, helping them make a buying decision on a home he had shown them. Becoming interested in his real estate business caused me to think about getting into real estate myself.

After five years of being married, our daughters still had not come to live with us. It felt as if it was time for me to consider doing something new. I had taught for 8 years. Maybe real estate?

I was a part-time stepmom, a wife, a teacher, but who was I? Still searching for my identity, a career change seemed to be the answer. Searching for purpose and why God made me, I was earnestly seeking to know His plan for my life.

One Saturday, I stopped by the real estate office where Terry was working part-time. I met a woman there that had been in the business many years. Her name is Jean. She was friendly, a few years older than me, and has a bubbly personality. Jean made me feel as if we'd known each other all of our lives, yet we just met.

"When are you going to join us in this real estate office?" Jean asked me.

"Maybe sooner than you think!" I answered, smiling.

Jean's invitation to come and work in real estate helped me with my decision to get my real estate license. Soon afterward, I signed up to take the real estate course to become a licensed realtor.

Passing the real estate course, the first time around was exciting. Yet taking the state exam, I failed by one point and felt devastated.

A visit home one Sunday helped me enormously. Dad's encouragement for me to retake the state exam made a significant impact. After visiting Dad, I went back home and scheduled the retake of my test. I was grateful for his advice.

Dad wasn't very present in our lives when we were younger, yet he related to us well when we were adults. It was comforting to share my disappointment with Dad. He told me how happy he was about my getting into real estate. His confirmation about my decision was helpful.

Retaking the test made an enormous difference that would affect the next twenty years of my life. I passed! Dad was thrilled, and so was I. We had a pleasant visit that weekend. Sadly, later that same year, Dad passed away. Although my Dad had his problems, our relationship in my adult years was very memorable. I truly love him and was saddened by his death at such a young age.

As a realtor entering the business world, God wanted to shape me in ways I could never have imagined. These years were learning and growing years for me, both professionally and personally. God took all of my successes and failures and used them for good.

At 29 and very naïve, my real estate career began. Young and never involved in the business world, this was unfamiliar territory for me. Filled with ambition and excitement to learn everything I could, the high-interest rates (18%) for home buying didn't bother me. Frankly, I didn't know any better.

Another personal goal for getting into real estate was to find a home for Terry and me to purchase. We had been renting for five years. Within my first year in the business, we were fortunate enough to find our first home.

This ranch home would be big enough for when the girls would come to live with us. It was within walking distance of Ewing High School, where Terry worked. The price was affordable, and the seller offered owner financing, making it possible for us to buy. It was perfect for us. We were thrilled. Some of the house's amenities were the brick working fireplace in the living room, finished basement, back screened porch, and remodeled kitchen. It was all on a treed lot. The front of the house was on a busy street, but the price was right, and all the other features made this a great first home for us.

Terry was pleased with my decision to get into real estate. He was most supportive and grateful we found a home of our own to purchase. We both knew that real estate could be all-consuming. I threw myself wholeheartedly into my new career. With all there was to learn as a new associate, my efforts to get up and running took some time.

Terry stopped doing real estate once I started my real estate career. He continued to teach, coach, and head up the Teacher's Association. He was supportive of my efforts to work hard and become successful.

Soon after starting work at the family-owned real estate office where I met Jean, our manager, Mike, told us he was moving to an office in Princeton, about twenty minutes north of our current office. Mike invited Jean and me to join him at his new office. Both of us enjoyed working with Mike. He kept us laughing with his self-deprecating humor, and he was an excellent manager.

To join the new office in Princeton, we had to meet with the broker, Jack, to interview. Jack was a friendly man, and after he asked Jean and me some questions, we had our opportunity to ask him our questions. Shortly after the interview, Jack invited us to join the company. Jean and I were thrilled, as was our manager, Mike.

Working in Princeton with its rich history and campus of Princeton University was exciting. It was a privilege. The school drew people from all over the world there. Our office was on the main road, Nassau Street, which was directly across from Princeton University. The name of our new company was Fox and Lazo. It was a step up for all of us, especially our clients. We had many more services to offer them to invest and sell their real estate.

Our multi-office company had an excellent relocation program, a mortgage company, professional marketing, experienced sales associates. Also, our company had a great salesperson training program for new associates. This was perfect for me, being a new salesperson. I immediately signed up for the company training.

The challenge to become productive quickly was energizing. It would be an opportunity to help my clients with one of their most significant investments, and I wanted to be as knowledgeable as possible to serve them best.

Unlike what happened in teaching, I didn't have to worry about people asking when Terry and I would start our family. Our office associates were always focusing on business.

Rarely did we have time to get involved in personal conversations. My MRKH would not be a problem here. Working as a realtor every day was different. I learned a great deal daily by listening to and by observing the experienced top sales associates in our office. In real estate, it was easy to stay busy. Busyness was always one of my coping strategies for my MRKH. When I'm busy or focused on something else, I can't be sorrowful.

Learning my new business, I was also searching for my identity and purpose in life. Not being a full-time mother, I believed that being a smart businesswoman was God's plan for my life. I approached my new career with mega ambition and personal expectations.

A speaker by the name of Tom Hopkins offered a professional real estate seminar nearby. It was my first real estate seminar I attended. Tom Hopkins was funny, engaging, and taught great techniques and dialog to use in our business. I bought his books and tapes and put his material he taught into use right away. It worked! His seminar birthed in me a desire to do public speaking myself someday. It was clear he had a lot of fun speaking, and he was a pro.

The thought of doing public speaking myself one day was a surprise to me. How could that be? I had a fear of public speaking. While working in real estate, I worked on my fear of public speaking by attending Toastmasters International and later the Dale Carnegie course. These were both challenging and helpful. I gained confidence in public speaking, which was useful later when I managed offices and conducted agent training for the company.

As an associate, I became motivated by the competition in real estate. Our company taught us to set goals each year.

We presented our plans to our office manager or broker. My goals and dreams had to be in writing, measurable and specific. It was beneficial setting goals and putting a plan in place to achieve them. My new career was exciting and off to a great start.

Our company encouraged our office to meet our goals by awarding levels of production once a year at a conference with all the agents from all of our branch offices in attendance. It was the annual awards breakfast. The award's breakfast, always held in a large convention center in a city nearby, was a big celebration. We all looked forward to it and car-pooled to get there. Year after year, these conferences are a celebration of the individual and office successes. Usually, awards are presented to associates one on one by the President of the company. It feels good to be appreciated for the hard work. The award's breakfasts were motivational.

Over the years, the incentives of increased income and award recognition kept me focused. I remember how I yearned to be the best salesperson. One of my first goals was to be the top producer in my office. Getting this award was a huge goal for a new associate. Amazingly, somehow, I became the leading agent in my office in my third and fifth year. Praise God!

My joy for achieving recognition as the best salesperson in my office was short-lived. I wondered why, since it was my focus for quite a while. It made little sense. I'd then go on to the next goal. I realized that awards and achievements never fulfilled my yearning to find my identity. Awards and all, I felt empty.

Success had a price called time. I worked seven days a week. My days, weeks, and months were full and caused me to miss valuable family time with my girls and husband. Missing precious family time was too high a price to pay for success. In hindsight, I see clearly. As the expression goes, "hindsight is 20/20." Although the girls were still not living with us, I still missed out on time with them.

My success became like a busyness addiction. I became my job and lived and breathed real estate. My accomplishments were ways to label myself (by an award level or title/new position, etc.) Yet again, it did not fill the identity void. I believe the term "workaholic" applied to me.

From 1980, during my real estate career to the early 1990s, I held several positions within the real estate field. My job became an addiction, an escape from MRKH. In those years, I went from a sales associate, promoted to manager, to regional director of recruiting with another company and again management for that company in Princeton. Also, I was a trainer at both company's corporate centers once a month while holding management positions.

All my work, success, and striving left me exhausted and empty. As I was climbing the ladder of success, I'd get to the top of the ladder and think: Nope, this is not it. I wasn't sure what "it" was that I was looking for. I was successful by the world's standards, but I didn't feel fulfilled in a profound, meaningful way. It felt like I had a hole in my heart.

Trying to find my identity and worth in work left my soul feeling empty. I continued to stuff my MRKH emotions. My poor self-image, a result of my childlessness, got worse—the part of "not fitting in with others" also still plagued my mind. No one knew.

Still uncertain about complications with MRKH, no further information, and never knowing if I'd ever meet someone else like me was excruciating, worrisome, and isolating. Day after day, I kept a smile on my face, hoping answers would come. For now, work was my escape.

I also dealt with my sorrow and stress when Terry and I socialized with friends; drinking alcohol was part of our social life. While drinking, I realized it helped me cope with my sorrow and exhaustion. It numbed my feelings. Sometimes Terry and I drank at home. Within a few years, the drinking at home increased, and I became concerned, worried about Terry's drinking, in particular. I considered myself a social drinker at this point.

Our drinking became problematic, and we separated for a while. Confusion filled me every day. Not knowing what to do, I was in survival mode. On weekends, I made trips to see my family at the shore. I saw Lori and Kim once in a while. Being separated from Terry, I didn't seek an attorney or anything. I just found a place to live with a friend to share expenses with and kept working. I stayed in touch with Terry and the girls.

After we were apart for some time, Terry got sober. We dated back together and in time, reunited. He became involved in a group called Alcoholics Anonymous aka A.A. Seeing Terry as a sober person was a massive change in him I didn't think I'd ever see. We reunited under the same roof. It was wonderful. Once we were back together, I had an "ah-ha" revelation for myself.

Being back with Terry as a completely sober person, I realized my drinking wasn't social; it was more. Sometimes we're so focused on someone else's problem, we don't see our own. The word for this is denial. I was in denial. The realization that I had a drinking problem was easily masked compared to when Terry drank. With the backdrop of

Terry's sobriety, I came to understand I was more than a social drinker. Soon, I too joined A.A. and we were both in the A.A. program and began living a sober life, one day at a time.

While we were apart, Lori and Kim finally came to live with Terry. By this time, the girls were high school age, and would attend Ewing High, where Terry was a teacher. I was glad they were living with their dad, in the first home we bought.

I still visited the girls and enjoyed spending time with them. I was grateful that they were my stepdaughters. Lori and Kim handled our separation reasonably well. I'm sure they felt relieved when Terry and I both became sober and were together again. It was as though we had a fresh start.

After graduating, the girls were off and into their own worlds. Lori had a boyfriend, Jimmy. They married. Kim went down the shore by my sister initially. She would later marry and move to Tennessee.

My beautiful
daughters,
Lori (left)
Kim (right)

Climbing the ladder of success, I became the manager of my office. I held this position for two years. I actually realized management was not for me. Thus, I sought employment elsewhere.

A competitor, Weichert Reality, hired me for their Princeton office to recruit sales associates. They appointed me as their Regional Director of Recruiting for Mercer County. It was a great opportunity and the most fun job I ever had.

Part of seeking to have a sales associate join our company was to meet with them, usually over lunch or coffee to see how they were feeling about where they were currently working. Once I understood what was working or not working well, I'd explain to them the benefits of joining Weichert Realty.

While at Weichert, a year later, they offered me the management position for their Princeton office. I took the job, yet shortly after realized, again, that management wasn't a fit for me. After a full year, Terry and I moved to Florida.

CONTEMPLATE & CONSIDER

❖ Unhealthy coping strategies, although giving temporary relief, are not a solution. Are you currently using an unhealthy escape?

_____
_____
_____
_____
_____
_____
_____

❖ What better strategies can you implement that will help you move forward in a healthier direction?

_____
_____
_____
_____
_____
_____
_____

Friend, it takes courage to put down the burdens from your past—especially if they've become part of your identity. But if you're wise, you will release them to the Father so He can set you free from the bondage they cause and make you whole.

— Charles Stanley

7

OUR FLORIDA INVESTMENT,
OUR FUTURE HOME

My friend, Jean (that worked with me in Princeton) lived six months in New Jersey and six months in Florida. One day Jean mentioned she purchased a bigger condo in the St. Pete Beach Yacht and Tennis Club, where they lived in Florida. We had visited Jean and her family in Florida and loved their place. Their condo was amazing. It was a seventh floor, corner unit, and had an incredible water view up the Intracoastal Waterway.

Immediately, I asked her, "Are you selling your other condo?"

Jean answered, "Yes, we are selling our condo, but just not right away. The penthouse we bought is being remodeled."

Instantly, my wheels started turning. I thought, *I wonder if Terry and I could buy Jean's condo. That would be great.* I asked Jean about her asking price. Once I gathered all the information, I went home to talk it over with Terry. He was pretty excited about the possibility of purchasing her condo as well. We thought about it for several days. The idea of moving to sunny Florida someday was enticing.

Terry and I told Jean we wanted to purchase her condominium. We gave her an offer, which she gladly accepted. We worked out all the details. When I think about how this all went together for all parties involved, it was as if it was meant to be. We hugged and celebrated our decision. Jean, her sisters, and mom were like family to us. We were thrilled.

Eventually, we would move to Florida full time. In the interim, we would rent it during the peak rental time (winter) to help us carry the cost. Jean recommended a couple from Canada that rented at her complex every year. Their names were Jim and Marie.

Once we closed on the condo, we did a few renovations to the inside. Jim and Marie became our winter tenants. With our renovations, they considered it to be like a honeymoon condo. They sent us their rent check with a letter explaining how much they loved living in our home. We enjoyed receiving their letters. Jim's letters increased our desire to move there ourselves. Three years in a row they rented and took excellent care of our place. When we moved to Florida, Jim and Marie found another rental. They were great tenants for us and now were neighbors and friends.

It was 20 years after my diagnosis, and still I never met one other woman with MRKH, and never met a doctor that knew about MRKH. I thought I might die and never meet someone else that was born with what I had. The aloneness of MRKH brings its own kind of grief, even amid otherwise joyful events. I still took one day at a time. My secret was intact. Every so often, triggers would send me into a season of depression.

Thankfully, Florida helped me with the bright sunshine, warm weather, and all it offered. Our new location was just what I needed. My depression was less with the beauty Florida offered: breathtaking sunrises, magnificently painted sunsets, white sandy beaches, palm trees, flowers in bloom all year round. The views of the Intracoastal Waterway, the

Gulf of Mexico, and the variety of beautiful birds added to the awe-inspiring nature that makes Florida what it is.

All this reminds me of how amazing God is to make the beauty and diversity in our world. Taking in the surrounding sights each day confirmed my belief in God, our Creator. He never left me, even though I had gotten so busy at work in New Jersey and was about to get busy again in Florida. He remained by my side through my sadness with MRKH. He moved me to a more beautiful part of His world. Our new home/condo was on the same street as our Catholic Church. I realized how much I missed going. Returning to church on Sundays felt good.

Early on, Terry realized the job he transferred with would not work out in Florida, so he left it. He and I went into real estate together. We joined Coldwell Banker Residential Real Estate, a large multi-office company. We worked in the St. Pete Beach office. I went full throttle into my work again, just like in New Jersey. I still hadn't found my identity and didn't think I would.

The challenge of learning a new market kept my mind work-oriented and busy. Like learning real estate when I was a new salesperson in New Jersey, learning the Florida market was a healthy distraction for my emotions connected to MRKH. Patty Pate, our office manager, gave us tips on working real estate in this area. Real Estate sales differed in Florida compared to selling real estate up north. In Florida we sold second homes or vacation homes versus people's primary residence. It was more of a "want market" than a "need market", especially on the beaches.

Patty warned us of the difficulty of the Florida market and helped us adjust to it. She was knowledgeable and helpful. With having done management in New Jersey, I knew how difficult Patty's job was. She was a true professional. Terry and I had a great deal of respect for Patty and the way she managed the office. She was an excellent coach, leader and friend.

Within a few years, the Coldwell Bank Clearwater Office needed a manager. Patty suggested Terry apply for the job. Terry interviewed with Mike Good, the CEO of West Central Florida. Mike hired Terry as the manager of Clearwater. Although Terry had never managed in real estate, Mike knew of Terry's success as a coach when he taught school. He was sure Terry would be a good fit for the job. Mike's estimation of Terry's ability to manage was accurate. Terry took the position and was successful with the Clearwater Office. It was a great fit. I had always told Terry I thought he'd make a great real estate manager. He did, and he enjoyed his position.

With Terry managing in Clearwater, I continued my personal business in the St. Pete Beach office. With focus and determination, I earned the different levels of clubs and awards based on income as I did in New Jersey.

As could have been predicted, I missed my family up north. Yet, good things happened. In our first year in Florida, my oldest brother, Al, and his wife, Judy, came for a visit. What a fun time we had together. We enjoyed the pool, beaches and lots of excellent restaurants. We went to St. Armand's Circle in Sarasota and had a delicious seafood dinner and enjoyed walking around afterward. St. Armand's Circle is filled with quaint shops, stores, galleries and more. The weather was perfect; we had ice cream and people watched as we enjoyed each other.

Al and Judy's favorite part of their visit was relaxing at our pool. Terry and I were extremely happy they vacationed with us. Al was fun to be around and the best big brother a girl could ever have. We had lots of fun with both of them.

While on vacation with us, Al and Judy showed their understanding and flexibility, when one night, I had to leave them to go write a contract at a condo on the beach. Not only did they not mind that I left them, Al told me how proud he was of the work I was doing. Al's words encouraged me a great deal.

We were sad to see Al and Judy depart when their vacation ended, but grateful to have had our time together. When they were with us, I felt like we were on vacation too, even though we worked here and there. We enjoyed good quality time together.

Over the years we lived in St. Pete Beach, we had memorable times with our girls and their families when they came for visits as well. The years between 1990 and 1995, Lori and Kim became moms themselves and Terry and I became grandparents. With the birth of each of our grandchildren, I felt blessed. Not being able to have children myself, yet having two daughters and in time, five beautiful grandchildren was extremely special to me. Our girls are wonderful moms. We are so proud of them.

Lori had three children: Ashley, James and Brianna and Kim had two boys: Jack and Michael. The grandchildren called Terry, Pop and me, G-ma. I was a young, grateful G-ma. I was 39 years old when our first granddaughter, Ashley, was born. Later, when she got older and came for a visit, she started calling me "Gigi" So to Ashley, I'm Gigi.

I loved when my granddaughters visited, one at a time. It was special to have our one-on-one time together. When Ashley or Brianna came for a visit, we had fun girl time together shopping, swimming, and going out to lunch. It was usually in the summer the girls visited, and we shopped for some back-to-school clothes.

Lori's family visited us from New Jersey and Kim's family, from Tennessee. It was always a fun family reunion. Since the girls lived in two different states, being able to see each other and us, created many precious memories. We would go to places like Disney World, Sea World, Busch Gardens in Tampa, the beaches, or just simply hang around the pool. All the kids loved visiting us in Florida. Everyone enjoyed the warm sunny weather.

Lori, Kim & kids at Busch Gardens for Christmas vacation.

Because everyone could not fit in our condo, Terry and I rented a place for the girls and their families to stay in together. They'd always be nearby. They enjoyed having their own place and being with each other. The kids were not only cousins, but good friends as well. We loved that they often made Florida their vacation destination. Our work offered us a flexible lifestyle, which allowed us to enjoy spending time with the kids when they came.

Terry managing the Clearwater office was a wonderful opportunity, which led to another position later on.

About eight years later Patty, my manager, was contemplating retirement. She recommended Terry to be interviewed for her position. Her office was one of the top offices in West Central Florida. Terry was thankful for Patty referring him to be considered for her position. He was hired. I was happy for Terry, yet sad to see Patty go. She deserved the time to relax in retirement.

I was still working in St. Pete Beach. With Terry getting hired to manage, it was time for me to take some time off. I had worked the past twenty years straight in real estate between New Jersey and Florida. I believed this was a good time for me to take a break, Terry agreed. In addition, there were other reasons, I wanted time to see my family up north.

In our years in St. Pete Beach, we had some sad news about our parents. Both Terry's and my mom had Alzheimer's disease. Our hearts were broken to know what Mom and Rose had to face at the end of their lives.

CONTEMPLATE & CONSIDER

❖ Have you been able to juggle a geographic move while suffering grief?

_____
_____
_____
_____
_____
_____
_____

❖ Did relocating help you? How?

_____
_____
_____
_____
_____
_____
_____

8

FAMILY VISITS TO NEW JERSEY

My mother's disease progressed after we had been in Florida a while. When I stopped working, I made frequent trips to see my family. Since I didn't live there, we all tried to get together when I visited. Sometimes it was difficult, but we did our best.

With Mom's Alzheimer's disease, she required round-the-clock care. The day my family brought Mom to the nursing home, I was there for a visit. I went with my brother, Al and my sister Mare, to take her. It was one of the saddest days of my life. Even with Mom's confusion, she knew she didn't want to stay there. It broke our hearts to see her reaction. Bringing Mom to live at the nursing home was traumatic and one of the most difficult things I've ever done. Visiting her was sad and heartbreaking. My siblings faithfully went to see her often. This is when being in Florida was difficult for me. I too visited each time I was in N.J. I was always happy seeing Mom, yet sad for her situation, I trusted it was best for her.

I've heard Alzheimer's disease referred to as: "the long goodbye," and that it is. Mom lived in the nursing home for quite a few years. When Mom was passing away, I didn't feel strong enough to see her take her last breath. My family called me to come up there, but I just couldn't. Looking back, it is one of my greatest regrets. I wish I went to say, "Goodbye," and tell Mom how much I loved her. I didn't feel able to handle it emotionally. Mom was a wonderful mom, and I loved her. Oh, how much I was going to miss her! Her death was surreal. Each day I wanted to call her, only to realize I couldn't. I went up to New Jersey for her funeral. I already missed her enormously and still do.

One of my favorite remembrances I have of Mom is as a younger girl and still living at home. Every once in a while, she and I would have a hot cup of tea together late at night. My older siblings were already out of the home and my younger brothers were sleeping. It was our special time. We talked about everything as we sipped our yummy warm tea. I cherish these memories.

Bobby, my younger brother, lived with Mom and had taken great care of her to the best of his ability. After Mom's passing, Bobby could not live by himself and eventually moved into a local nursing home too. Bobby suffered from mental illness. Thankfully my sister, Barbara, worked hard to place Bobby into a very good local nursing home where he was happy. He liked it so much he tried to convince us to move in there too. Bobby was so sweet. He was very family oriented and had a beautiful heart.

He was well loved at his nursing home. Bobby was like the mayor there. He had a unique gift of perception. When we'd visit Bobby, he could tell if something was going on in our life, before we even mentioned it. He was amazing, lovable and a joy to visit. He always enjoyed the coffee and bagel with cream cheese or other goodies we'd bring him. After a while Bobby became immobile. He would need a wheelchair to get around. He did pretty well with it. He went all around the nursing home on his new chair.

Bobby and my youngest brother, Joey, were closest in age. They were best buddies. To watch them converse with each other was so funny. They had their very own language. They'd end up laughing that each could understand the other. It was funny to see them do this. Bobby and Joey were close in more than just age. He loved when Joey frequently visited him after work and/or on weekends. Sadly, Bobby, like Dad, died in his early sixties.

Terry's mom, Rose, was in a nursing home as well. Ed kept her home as long as possible. Like my mom, Rose needed round-the-clock care. Ed took Rose up to Kansas, near where his oldest son, Ed and his wife Kaye lived. Ed lived with them while Rose was in the home there. We went to Kansas many times to see Rose and Ed, and Eddie and Kaye.

When Rose passed away, Ed came to live with us full time in Florida, in 1998. He was comfortable in Florida. He was quite a character. Ed and I got along well. He was like a dad to me. He was in his 90s when he came to live with us. He was mellow as an older man, compared to his younger years when he was pretty cantankerous.

With Ed living in our two-bedroom condo with us for three years, Terry and I thought it might be good to get a bigger place to live. We both felt we needed more room. One day, while riding around, we passed a For Sale by Owner sign in front of a house on Park Street in St. Petersburg. We wrote the number down and called it later. Once we connected with the seller, we discovered it was possibly affordable for us to purchase.

The house was magnificent. We made an appointment to see it. The home wasn't on the water, but it was huge. There was enough space to have all our children: daughters, husbands and grandchildren come and stay with us. For my father-in-law, it had a master suite with a full bath on the first floor. Selling our waterfront condo that we owned for over ten years, allowed us to make the purchase of this larger home. Our condo had increased in value.

Our first Christmas in our big new home was memorable. We could have both of our daughters and their families come and stay with us. What fun we had being under one roof. The home had an in-ground pool that everyone enjoyed. Lori, Kim, and their families saw Ed for the first time in many years, and it was a reunion for all of them. Ed got to be with Lori, Kim and his five great-grandchildren.

Sadly, Ed passed away the second year we were in this home. Now our home felt larger than ever without Ed living with us. I missed Ed terribly. With my Mom and Terry's moms passing away, and now Ed, it really made me think about how precious life is. It goes by quickly.

Not long after losing Ed, we received devastating news about my brother Al. He was diagnosed with Primary Progressive Aphasia. Al slowly lost his ability to speak, communicate and even write. His frustration with not being able to communicate became more difficult as his illness progressed. His decline was gradual.

Al and Judy, and Barbara and Joe, came to visit us in our new home. We had the best time together. Each couple had their own bedroom and bath. We'd meet downstairs in the kitchen for breakfast in the morning. With Al's illness, we realized how precious our time together was and made the most of it. Al knew about his condition and could still communicate well at this point. We did very little running around. We had the pool, a few meals out, and just relaxed. Terry and I were happy they could come for a visit. When everyone went home, Terry and I were once again lost in our big house.

With almost everyone having visited us during our few years in this home, and Ed's passing away, we thought about selling it. The memories we made, we'll never forget. The big house was pleasant to share with family, but now seemed too big for just the two of us.

As an office manager, Terry took trips with Coldwell Banker. His office was the top office for the company. Meetings were always out of state. When he was away, the house felt even bigger with just me in it. This is when I'd visit my family in New Jersey. Shortly after Ed's passing, we sold the house and moved back into a condo on the water.

I adopted a little Shitzu dog named Lizzy from the shelter. She was 3 years old and a beautiful addition to our lives. She truly was our baby dog. When we first got her, she was timid and shy. In no time at all she was a confident, cheerful dog. Terry and I loved Lizzy being with us. I took Lizzy to New Jersey with me each time I went. She traveled well. I think God allows us to have dogs in our lives to bring extra love and healing. Lizzy was like our child. We frequently spoiled her. She was our little princess, and she acted that way.

Within that year, with visiting my family so frequently in New Jersey, Terry and I purchased a second home, a townhouse in an area called Smithville. My brother Joey helped us offset our expenses by renting it. I'd be able to come to N.J. and stay in my place and come often. Joey and I enjoyed our visit when I'd be up there to see everyone. He always makes me laugh, just like my brother, Al.

CONTEMPLATE & CONSIDER

❖ Our little Lizzy added so much to our lives, do you have a four-legged fur baby? How can he or she be a source of healing?

_____

_____

_____

_____

_____

_____

_____

❖ Family and friends are sources of healing. Write how siblings, aunts, nieces, nephews, etc. have brought joy and comfort into your life.

_____

_____

_____

_____

_____

_____

_____

9

IDENTITY FOUND – HALLELUJAH

Searching for truth and my identity, my life improved greatly. On one of my visits to New Jersey, I had a life-changing experience on May 29, 2003. My sister Mare and her husband Dave invited me to come to their new church with them.

Everyone in my family was raised Catholic, yet Mare and Dave changed to a Baptist church near their home. I was curious about their new church because they were extremely happy with it. At first, I didn't understand why she and Dave left the Catholic Church.

The Sunday I visited their church, Trinity Baptist, I noticed right away that the atmosphere was inviting. All the people were happy to be there. Many hugged each other as though they were family members. The young pastor that Mare introduced me to, Pastor Steve, was enthusiastic and glad to meet me. Talking with him, he spoke as though he knew Jesus personally. Pastor Steve quickly praised Jesus in our conversation several times. His spirit of hospitality and joy made me feel welcome.

In my home church, few people spoke with each other before Mass. Everyone entered the church, sat down, and waited for the priest to come out. There was little talk among the people. The only time Jesus was mentioned was from the pulpit, rarely in conversation.

Once the service began, I saw how different this church was from my church. The words of the songs were projected up to the front so we could sing along. The worship team was excellent. The lyrics of the songs were beautiful and unlike any songs I've ever heard. They ushered us into the presence of God. The entire experience was less formal, and extremely impactful. As the congregation sang, their love and joy of the Lord filled the atmosphere all the more.

There were no candles, no statues, and no stained-glass windows. The pastor wore regular clothing, not vestments. The sermon Pastor Steve shared opened my heart to truth I never knew before. This church, although not what I was used to, was relatable and understandable. The pastor's prayers were heartfelt and real, like he was speaking directly with Jesus Christ in a personal and loving way. There were no rote prayers that we had to respond to. All of it: the friendly congregation, the worship songs, the sermon, the prayers and atmosphere opened my heart in a way I wasn't expecting. Yet, it all made perfect sense. I felt comfortable, welcome and at home in this church.

I heard the pastor say, *"All have sinned and fall short of the glory of God."* Wow, I thought, these people don't think they are all perfect. What I didn't realize at the time was that the words he spoke were from the Bible (Romans 3:23 NIV). Next the pastor said, *"For the wages of sin is death, but the gift of God is eternal life in Christ Jesus our Lord"* (Romans 6:23 NIV).

I learned that day: all people have sinned, we're born with sin. And that the payment for our sin is death, yet the gift of eternal life is offered through belief in God's son, Jesus Christ, whose death on the cross paid the price for all of our sins. We are saved by "**grace**" not "**works**."

In my Catholic faith, I remember being taught eternal life was through "works." I loved hearing that salvation is a *gift* from God. We only have to believe and receive it by saying a simple prayer. It's called the Gospel, which means "Good News," and that is what it was to me, good news!

At the end of service, Pastor Steve asked if we'd like to receive Christ as our Lord and Savior that day. He asked us to bow our heads and say a simple prayer from our hearts after him. It went like this:

> *Father God, I confess my sins and believe Jesus took the punishment I deserved when He died on the cross and rose to life three days later. I receive Jesus into my heart and life to be my Lord and Savior. I repent of my sins. Help me to live for You, by the power of Your Holy Spirit. In Jesus's name I pray. Amen*

After saying the prayer, Pastor Steve asked us to raise our hands if we prayed to receive Jesus into our hearts. I raised my hand that day and became a Christian. I was 52 years old. This is a day I will never forget. I gave my life to Christ and was adopted into God's family. I found my identity...Praise God! Now I was a daughter of the King of kings and Lord of lords. The hole in my heart was full. Unknown to me, all the years of searching for my identity, my heart was actually seeking Jesus. I left church that day a whole new person.

The Bible says, *"Therefore, if anyone is in Christ, the new creation has come: The old has gone, the new is here!"* (2 Corinthians 5:17 NIV). My life changed from that day on. When I take my last breath here on earth, I am raised to eternal life in heaven with Jesus. While here on earth, He transforms our life. What a beautiful promise.

Pastor Steve told us that Trinity Baptist Church had a gift for all those who gave their life to Christ. We were to pick it up in the back of the church after service. I felt joy and peace. The words I heard at Trinity Baptist Church changed my life forever. I was grateful to my sister Mare and her husband Dave for inviting me to their church and also for their prayers for me.

The gift the church gave us was a small New Testament New Believer's Bible. I was excited to have a Bible, it was my first one. When I went home, I read my new Bible cover to cover. I couldn't put it down. I was starving for the truth found in God's Word. I feasted on it. In the beginning of this Bible were questions new believers have, and it gave the scripture and page number where to find it to see the answer. I learned so much by reading it.

I was no longer lost, I was found. Adopted into the family of God, I became a Christian. The Bible became my life instruction manual, my love letter from God. My heart was on fire for Jesus. It was great being assured I was going to heaven when I died. My burning desire was to learn how to share the Good News with others so they too could have eternal life and a new life in Christ, especially all my loved ones.

If you'd like to receive Christ into your heart like I did, pray the prayer on page 85. Tell someone what you did and share your good news. It is never too late to receive Jesus. When you pray the prayer from your heart, you too will have eternal life in heaven and begin a personal relationship with Jesus.

The Bible says, "*If you declare with your mouth, 'Jesus is Lord,' and believe in your heart that God raised him from the dead, you will be saved. For it is with your heart that you believe and are justified, and it is with your mouth that you profess your faith and are saved*" (Romans 10:9 NIV).

In Florida, soon after I got home, I bought my first full Bible with the Old and New Testament. I purchased the NLT version of the Bible. NLT means New Living Translation. This Bible is easy to understand as a new Christian. The bottom of each page has paragraphs helping readers to understand what the Bible verses mean.

The biggest difference after receiving Christ into my heart when compared to my Catholic faith is, I now have a personal relationship with Jesus. My faith is a "relationship" not a "religion."

When I said that the pastors at Trinity Baptist all seemed like they knew Jesus personally, they did. So did the church members. I could sense and see the love and joy of the Lord in everyone. I'm forever grateful for my relationship with Christ.

Ever since that day, my desire to know and love God more continues to grow ever stronger. The Bible is the best way to do that. I got involved in Bible study groups at a new church at home in Florida, and I read God's Word every day. The Bible is my most valuable possession. I consider my Bible, a life instruction manual, written and inspired by God, Himself.

Upon returning home, I searched for a Christian Church and found Indian Rocks Baptist Church. On my first visit, I knew it would be my church. It had the same atmosphere as my sister's church. Everyone was friendly. I was thrilled!

Terry wasn't sure what was going on and why I wanted to find a new church. In my enthusiasm for the greatest thing that ever happened to me, I tried to explain how I became a Christian, and shared the Good News to Terry. He had been Catholic his entire life and wasn't ready to make a change.

He tried to understand and clearly saw my joy about my new faith. I asked Terry if he minded if I joined the church in Indian Rocks.

He said, "No, he didn't mind." He saw my joy for becoming a Christian and knew how important it was that I find a church to go to. I love his being able to be okay with this change for me.

Occasionally, I went with Terry to the Catholic Church as well. I missed going to church with him. He was okay with me joining Indian Rocks Baptist church, and he came there with me sometimes as well. Indian Rocks had a Saturday night "country church" service, with the worship music all country music. Terry liked that a lot, he enjoys country music. I loved when Terry came to church with me.

I prayed from the day I joined Indian Rocks Church that Terry would one day become a Christian and we would go to church together again. Many of my new Christian friends joined me and prayed this prayer for us too. Having friends that prayed with me was something I never had before.

I attended Christianity 101 and several other classes at my new church. It was comforting to learn and grow in my faith. In my excitement to share the Gospel, I couldn't wait to attend a class called Evangelism Explosion, teaching us how to share the Gospel. It was excellent. Part of this class was evangelizing people who visited our church. This was an amazing experience and opportunity to grow. It equipped us to share the Gospel with others.

With my joy of being a Christian, it was as if my dark days of depression and isolation from my MRKH, were being infused daily by the light and love of my Lord and Savior, Jesus Christ. Having a personal relationship with

Jesus filled my heart to overflowing. His love for me overwhelmed me in a good way, I was being transformed.

After striving twenty years in real estate and seeking my identity, when I received Christ, I knew *who I was* and *whose I was*. I was a daughter of the King of kings and Lord of lords. Jesus saw my sorrow, strife, and searching. I found my identity the day I became a Christian. My new life brought revived energy, happiness, and hope I hadn't known before. I was forgiven, free, and adopted into the family of God.

Excited to have a whole new life, I found a scripture one day that said, *"Be still and know that I am God"* (Psalm 46:10 NIV). These words were and are today very meaningful after my twenty years of working, striving, and seeking. This scripture is personal for me.

MRKH was still my secret, but now the difference was the love that was in my heart. The love of Jesus made all the difference. My new life in Christ was exciting and I could find comfort reading His Word, the Bible. There are over 3,000 promises in the Bible. I also had a sense of confidence that I didn't have before. I had the Spirit of God within me.

The following year my brother Al passed away. His struggle with Primary Progressive Aphasia ended. By the grace and strength of God, I could be with Al, his wife, Judy, and the family when Al took his last breath. We miss Al terribly, love him, and believe we'll see him again in heaven. He lives on in our hearts and minds as well.

On Sundays after church, while attending Bible study, I met JoAnn, a Christian for many years. She became my spiritual mentor and good friend. JoAnn was patient as I learned and grew in my faith. She's a great encourager.

At Jo Ann and her husband Dave's home, I attended a study on the book: The Purpose Driven Life by author, Rick Warren. This study helped us to discover purpose through God's Word. I highly recommend reading this book. I've reread it several times and later led a study of it myself. It is a book I enjoy rereading.

My life, now so full and busy, was not exhausting. I was building relationships with my Lord and my brothers and sisters in Christ. My life was enriched beyond description.

While at Indian Rocks, I took my first mission trip to Brazil in 2009. It was with a team from my church. What a new experience! Never would I believe I'd be brave enough to go to another country without my husband. Terry was proud of me for going on the mission trip and was supportive with my planning to go.

Terry told me later that my bravery to go on a mission trip out of the country spoke volumes to him of the difference Jesus made in my life. I was happy to hear Terry say that. He told me that this was part of his believing how Christ can give us a whole new life. A short time later our prayers were answered. Terry believed and became a Christian.

With all I was learning and doing with my church, it was as though MRKH faded into the background. It was there, I would still have some depression when triggered, but now was believing God had a plan for me. I began feeling acceptance. In the meantime, my joy for the Lord Jesus kept me focused on what He was teaching me. This part of my life took precedence over my sorrow of MRKH. Yet, my secret was still intact.

Captured by Jesus's love, my life was and is changing to become the person God intended me to be. His transforming power will continue as I grow closer to Him and until I take my last breath here on earth. God is good.

As a new believer with my heart on fire for Jesus, while working at home I began writing poems. The poems were an outflow of what I was learning in my walk with Jesus and the overflow of my heart of love and gratitude. I saved the poems in a file and would pull them out and reread them. They ministered to me.

Wanting to share my poems with others, I often thought how nice it would be to publish them in a book. Not knowing how to do that, they stayed in my file drawer for quite some time. Whenever I wrote more poems, I added them to the file. Years later, my friend helped me to publish them. This was a dream come true. More on that in a future chapter.

"For God so loved the world that he gave his one and only Son, that whoever believes in him shall not perish but have eternal life" *(John 3:16 NIV)*.

Watercolor painting of Jesus
by: Julie

CONTEMPLATE & CONSIDER

❖ Who or what is your source of strength?

_____
_____
_____
_____
_____
_____
_____

❖ What evidences do you see in the world that helps
you believe that God exists?

_____
_____
_____
_____
_____
_____
_____

10

PARENTING GRANDCHILDREN
& A HEALING DISCOVERY

While in our Florida condo, our grandson, James visited us from New Jersey. We loved having him visit with us. When his vacation ended, James asked us if he could come to live with us and go to college in Florida. This took us by surprise. Terry and I discussed his idea and gave James a big "yes." We liked the idea. He took a flight to visit, he'd fly home and drive his car back to Florida. We talked with Lori, his mom, about James coming to live with us. She thought his moving in with us would be good for him. Our plan was in place. James went home and packed his things, then drove back to Florida.

In no time at all, we had our grandson living with us. We had an extra bedroom that was our office with a comfy pull-out Murphy bed, which became his bedroom. We were happy that he wanted to go to college. As soon as he could, he signed up for school and was off to a good start.

James also secured a job at Publix, our local supermarket on St. Pete Beach. He was thrilled with his new job and excited about school. He did both well. We were proud of him for getting his job to provide money for his living expenses.

James has a cheerful spirit and brought a lot of fun into our lives. All our neighbors knew James from seeing him in the elevator. He always wore his baseball cap on his head backwards, looked punky, but cute. Our neighbors loved

James. He was probably the youngest person living in the condo building. Everyone got a kick out of him. His red hair and freckles distinguished him and set him apart even more.

Being in a condo building with mostly older people wasn't fun for James. Since he was a country music fan, like Terry, I invited him to our Saturday Country Music service at church. While at church James met my friend, Dee. They enjoyed each other immediately. She is a cool lady, older than me, but her spirit is very young. Dee and James sat together in church and were like little kids. Hearing them giggling and goofing around, I sat between them like a mom to stop their crazy behavior. It was fun that they enjoyed each other.

At church, the youth pastor introduced James to kids his age. One night, they all went out. James was uncomfortable. The church kids differed from the city kids he knew from home. James made friends at work and school. As responsible grandparents, we told James the importance of "who" his friends were and the influence they could have on his life. We gave him our best advice in hopes he would embrace it.

When James came to live with us, he spoke with his cousin Jack in Tennessee each night via Skype. He encouraged Jack to come to Florida and live with us too and go to school in Florida. One day James asked us if Jack could come and stay with us as well. We talked with Kim, his mom, about Jack coming to live in Florida. Kim was fine with the idea as well. So, Jack would soon join us.

Jack and Jim were close in age, were cousins and good friends. We'd soon have to move because we didn't have another bedroom in the condo. Terry had been talking with me about moving someday to be able to consider retiring soon. With Jack coming, we had good reason to move. We made plans to purchase another home with more space.

Having the boys living with us was like being a mom, only the boys were college age, and I was their grandmother. Like motherhood, some days presented us with unique scenarios. They kept us going. We loved our time with our grandsons, and they gave our lives an extra dimension. I was doing more cooking, cleaning, and all of that mom stuff, but I didn't mind. Terry and I had many opportunities to laugh, love, coach, correct, and grow with our grandsons.

Terry took Jack and James to a few different outings with him. One particular time was a Ray's Baseball game that Terry's Coldwell Banker office went to. They all had a great time. The boys and Terry also had a chance to see Bruce Springsteen live in concert. Having them live with us, allowed these memorable times to happen.

Jack and James

We moved to a town called Ellenton to a new home with plenty of room. There were even two guest bedrooms. Yes, we were in another large home. When the boy's moms, our daughters, came for a visit, we had plenty of room. We had another wonderful Christmas in this home the first year as well.

This home was suitable for the season of life we were in. One thing Terry and I did well together, as I mentioned before, is move and set up house in no time at all. While there, my sister Barbara and her husband Joe and my brother Joey visited us when we lived in Ellenton. Also, our granddaughters Ashley and Brianna visited, the girls would come separately and stay for a week to ten days. We loved having family visit.

The great part about our grandsons and us being together was that we searched for a new church that we could all go to. I was thrilled the guys wanted to church shop with us. Terry and I would be back at church full time together. I believe Terry was ready for a Christian Church after spending those years visiting Indian Rocks Baptist Church.

We found a church called Bayside Community Church in Bradenton. After visiting several churches, I remember praying and asking God where He wanted us. That very day our grandson Jack told me he really wanted to join Bayside. We chose Bayside Community Church in Bradenton to be our new church. Jack's remark after church was my answered prayer. Having the boys attend church with Terry and I gave me hope that they'd have a good foundation in their lives. I am forever grateful for Jack's great choice of a church. We are blessed at Bayside.

One night I invited James to a meeting at our church called Celebrate Recovery. The group met once a week and was for people working on hurts, habits and hang-ups. It is a recovery program that teaches eight principles and twelve Christ centered steps. CR as this program is referred to, was started out of Saddleback Church where Rick Warren, author of: The Purpose Driven Life is the pastor. CR is in churches all over the country. My friend and hairdresser, Cindy was leading CR with her husband Dave at our church. She is the one who told me about CR. I brought James that night at her recommendation. She thought he would like it.

I thought attending CR would be helpful for James and that he might meet some guys that he could be friends with. He and I went to a meeting together. I enjoyed it, but I don't think James was interested at this point. Little did I know by bringing James to CR, God actually brought me to an amazing place to begin my healing with MRKH.

In Celebrate Recovery I learned and became free from my hurt in connection with MRKH. This all happened over a period of years. I was happy to have found a place I could finally openly share my lifelong secret sadness. God works in our lives in mysterious ways. I could never have imagined CR would be a meeting to help me.

It is kind of funny, in that many times people bring others for help to CR and end up staying just like me. It is an amazing program and just what I needed to help me deal with facing my fears of sharing how I was born. It felt like a very safe place and it was.

Being able to talk about MRKH released me from my self-imprisonment, emotions and the secret life of MRKH. My secret for 42 + years was released, and it was an enormous break-through for me. It was as good as having counseling. Over time, I had the privilege of sharing my testimony at our church and other campuses for Celebrate Recovery meetings. What a joy it is to share this "only God" story. I call this my story for His Glory.

The years our grandsons lived with us and attended school were a once in a lifetime experience. After graduation, Jack moved back home to Tennessee and found work. James remained in Florida and moved into a place with his friend. James worked as an air-conditioning repair person and salesman. He did very well in his new line of work and enjoyed it. My years with Jack and James gave me joy and a genuine appreciation for the job of motherhood. My grandsons were fun and sometimes a handful and they tested our limits, but still we were all the better for it.

Years later, we witnessed a miracle healing after a tragic motorcycle accident our grandson James was in. He was diagnosed with traumatic brain injury, also called a TBI. When this first happened, we were not sure he'd live. If he did, we were not sure if he would walk, talk, be able to drive or anything like that. He had brain surgery. He spent a full year in three different hospitals. Our family and James' girlfriend, Kelly, and her family all pulled together. Life was on hold.

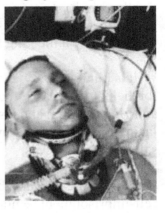

His recovery was slow and challenging. Lori and Kim worked well together to help James in various aspects of his recovery process. It took a team to handle it all, and they did an outstanding job.

Everyone organized an army of prayer warriors from every place possible. So many people prayed fervently for James to have a full recovery. After the three different hospitals, physical therapy, and lots of love and support from family and friends, James very gradually had his miraculous cure!

From the beginning of this experience to the end we saw God answering prayers and showing us His omnipotence (His being an all-powerful God). He was with us and never left us. In His timing, He gave us our miracle. Praise be to God!

Attitude — Changes Everything!

Update: James' recovery continues. We are grateful that James's attitude about his experience is amazing. He knows that God has a plan and a purpose for his survival and recovery. Even though he is unable to work, James hopes that someday he will have the opportunity to share his story and help others.

CONTEMPLATE & CONSIDER

❖ Are you aware of any recovery programs in your area? For me, Celebrate Recovery was a good fit and is offered in other areas.

_____

_____

_____

_____

_____

_____

_____

❖ You can experience motherhood through different means. What could yours be?

_____

_____

_____

_____

_____

_____

_____

11

A NEW LIFE WITH BAYSIDE

After our grandsons left, we sold our house in Ellenton and moved closer to our church. We downsized to a villa, a perfect size home for the two of us in retirement.

We had already joined Bayside Community Church. Bayside has a young congregation and we like that. We enjoy the younger people and know they will keep us young too. When our children and family come for a visit, they always love to come to Bayside. They enjoy our church and that makes Terry and I happy. A few of them watch Bayside on-line from where they live up in New Jersey and Tennessee.

The mission statement for our church is: Bayside Community Church exists to: Help People Know God, Find Family, Live in Freedom, and Discover Purpose. Terry and I are experiencing our church's mission statement personally, praise God! We are grateful for our Bayside Family. We enjoy all that we are learning from our pastoral staff and groups. We feel like we are living in freedom and have found our purpose.

One day when I was new at church, I was invited to someone's home that I didn't know. Her name is Gloria Brush. She was having a luncheon for me and two other women that I'd never met. They were Doretha Brown and Barbara Alpert. This luncheon was special. Gloria served us a delicious lunch of spareribs, salad and dessert and it was yummy. What fun we all had over lunch. We got to know each other well. There was never a lull in our conversation.

We came to Gloria's home that day as strangers and left as friends. What a special beginning to many wonderful years of fellowship, friendship, and family.

At lunch Barbara was telling us she just completed publishing her memoir: <u>Arise My Daughter, A Journey from Darkness to Light</u>. Her book tells of survival of childhood trauma and suicide attempts. She suffered from BDD. She tells in her story how God transformed her from a life of trauma into the life He destined her to have. Barbara's book helps others face their personal struggles and inner battles to find freedom and a new life as she did. Barbara credits the Lord for her freedom and transformation. Her story is phenomenal. It surely was an encouragement to me.

I identified with Barbara's book with my lifelong battle with MRKH. Barbara told us that day at our luncheon that her healing was due in part to writing her story. As I write my story, I am experiencing what Barbara experienced, a healing after many years, praise God. Once I read Barbara's memoir, it was the key that unlocked my prison door of secrecy with MRKH. It is amazing how God works things out like this.

Having met Barbara and realizing she was an author, I thought, *"Perhaps Barbara could help me publish my poems."* Remember the poems I was writing and saving in my drawer?

On our way out of Gloria's house that day, I asked Barbara how she published her book and told her about the poems I would like to publish. She graciously offered to help me. Several days later Barbara and I met so she could look at the poems. Once Barbara looked at them, she encouraged me to publish them. She offered to help me. I was thrilled and felt like Barbara was an angel sent from God. Seeing my poems published was something I didn't think I'd see in my lifetime. It was a dream come true.

Barbara led a Bayside women's group for authors called the Women's Writers Circle. She invited me to join. The small group was held at her home and I was excited to attend. The women were all working on their own stories. We met once a week and helped each other edit our work. This group met for many months. Everyone was an encouragement. It was fun to watch and experience each author's success being published. I felt honored to know and be a part of these dear sisters in Christ who were also authors. We became family and friends.

Barbara and I worked one on one also. Together we designed a cover for the poem book. We worked on the entire book for about nine months. Once done, <u>The King's Poems from God's Heart to Yours</u> was birthed! We were thrilled at its completion and delivery. Barbara, knowing about my MRKH, said, "Julie, you just gave birth to your first book." Her comment was sweet; it really did feel like that to me.

Doretha Brown, one woman at Gloria's luncheon, was also in Barbara's Women's Writer's Circle Group. She completed her book called: <u>Behind the Walls I Called Home.</u> Doretha's story is a precious memoir of her own childhood and life into adulthood and is a great read. We are all friends, church members, authors and grateful to do life together.

Years later, Doretha held a women's seminar titled: Women's Self-Awareness Conference at a local hotel and invited us to join her and to present our stories/books. I had the privilege to speak at her

conference and share my story and poem book. It was an honor to be one of her speakers and be a part of the authors and speakers there that evening.

Publishing the poem book, speaking at a conference, attending and leading groups in Celebrate Recovery, sharing my testimony of living with MRKH…felt as though God was giving me a life of beauty for ashes.

My earlier years of sorrow and isolation was transforming into a beautiful new life of joy. Life became fulfilling, different, open, and free. Finally, I had a life of purpose.

Today, I'm convinced that God had a plan for me all along. The Bible tells us: *"For I know the plans I have for you," declares the LORD, "plans to prosper you and not to harm you, plans to give you a hope and a future"* (Jeremiah 29:11 NIV).

A few months later, with the poem book I led two women's small groups for Bayside church. With our Bibles, a workbook, and The King's Poems from God's Heart to Yours, we focused on each poem's content using comparable scriptures and had wonderful Holy Spirit inspired discussions. These were two different groups. What a great way to have fellowship and fun!

When Terry and I initially joined Bayside Community Church, we served as greeters at our services. Later we led a co-ed group: Financial Peace University (a Dave Ramsey course), also known as FPU. Terry was the leader, and I was the co-leader. This course is an excellent program designed to help people with finances, budgeting, and getting out of debt. We led FPU for quite some time. Terry's background working in the financial industry gave him a desire to help others with finances. He is excellent in this area.

Eventually we led another co-ed group, called Securing Your Financial Future. This is when I realized God had a sense of humor. Finances were Terry's strength, passion and expertise, not mine. Maybe that's why God had me co-lead, for me to learn more about finances. Surprisingly, I eventually did. We had a number of these small groups.

Terry's passion also was now being filled to the brim since he loves helping people with financial matters. Our group, Securing Your Financial Future, was developed by Terry. His course covers three areas: 1.) Risk-Management 2.) Investments and 3.) Real Estate.

It is inspiring when we see people making good financial decisions for their families. Many people share with us some great personal successes they have with their finances because of our small group. It is humbling to hear their splendid news.

"And let us consider how we may spur one another on toward love and good deeds, not giving up meeting together, as some are in the habit of doing, but encouraging one another—and all the more you see the Day approaching."

Hebrews 10: 24-25 NIV

CONTEMPLATE & CONSIDER

❖ Do you have a place to connect with others?

_____
_____
_____
_____
_____
_____
_____

❖ Why do you think being connected to others is so important?

_____
_____
_____
_____
_____
_____
_____

12

FINDING MY MRKH SISTERS

The day came that we had a home computer. I could use my computer and finally Google, "What is MRKH?" I was in my early 60s. After a lifetime of questions, there would be answers. My isolation ended as I learned of others with MRKH. Finding MRKH sisters was amazing! I was excited to get information and understand more about my rare condition and meet others (even if online only). Finally, my world of isolation and despair was changing. It was possible to connect with women that had MRKH.

It would still take a while to feel free and accepting of my condition. Yet between my new life in Christ, Celebrate Recovery meetings at church, and learning about my MRKH Warrior sisters, another new world opened up. Life was changing in different ways than I ever imagined.

On the computer, I looked up MRKH and found a group of women that belong to BYMRKH, which stands for Beautiful You MRKH Foundation, Inc. It is founded by women with MRKH and exists to support and empower women with MRKH. It is an excellent organization (501C3). The President and CEO is Amy C. Lossie, Ph.D., and the Executive Director and Vice President is Christina Ruth. These ladies, through BYMRKH, continue to empower, inform, and bring MRKH Warriors together into a community where they can realize their strengths and encourage one another. Women's growth, acceptance, connection, and understanding are possible through the BYMRKH organization.

Finding BYMRKH was genuinely fantastic! On their page, there were faces of women that have MRKH. Why was this so impactful for me? Until this point, I'd never met or even heard of *one* other woman in the entire world that had MRKH. Just seeing their faces and knowing other women had MRKH, I was no longer alone. My one wish, to at least talk with or meet a woman with MRKH in person, was about to come true.

Looking online one day, advertised on another MRKH site, I saw a meet-up planned in the city of Philadelphia through Mid-Atlantic MRKH. My husband and I lived in Florida. I showed him the information, and we were both excited to go. It would be a group of women with MRKH, doctors, and others to speak to the attendees. First, there was a general meeting with speakers. Then there were break-out groups. All planned to make this an informative, fun day for women with MRKH and their families.

I called Meredith Brookes; the person leading the meeting in Philadelphia. I was nervous about making the call since I had never spoken to anyone with MRKH. Meredith was friendly and put me at ease immediately. She told me her MRKH story. We talked for quite a while. I told her she was my very first contact or voice of MRKH. She and I shared our MRKH stories; she answered questions and was a great listener. I asked her if I was too old to attend, being in my 60s.

Meredith emphatically said, "Absolutely not!" She encouraged me to come. It was comforting to speak to someone who understood me like no one else ever had. Speaking with Meredith made all the difference.

I told Terry, "I had the best conversation with a friendly person with MRKH, who made me feel welcome to come to the meeting in Philadelphia." I told him I wanted to attend. Terry agreed we should go. He is always empathetic to my lifelong search to know more about MRKH. He is and always has been my best support.

We made plans to fly to Philadelphia. Guess what: Philadelphia was the same city I learned of my diagnosis of MRKH 44 years earlier. Wow, this was full circle.

Arriving at the meeting, I met Amy Lossie from BYMRKH. What a pleasant surprise for me. I didn't realize she'd be at this meeting. I knew Amy from seeing her online. It was lovely to meet Amy in person and thank her for all her excellent work for MRKH women.

Since we took our dog, Lizzy, to Philadelphia with us, Terry could not come into the meeting with me. When Amy greeted me at the door with her beautiful, friendly smile, she said to me, "Julie, we are so happy you are here, welcome. I know it must be hard for you to come in. Take your time."

My response to Amy was, "Oh, Amy, it's not hard; I want to come in, please." I explained it had been so many years that I thought I would never meet another person like me. I couldn't wait to enter the room and meet my MRKH sisters. She understood, and we went in together.

I loved Amy's heart to encourage me to feel welcome and at home. Amy, Christina, and Meredith seemed like family immediately. I was so happy to meet them and be with all my young MRKH sisters. I was no longer alone. We all hugged like we knew each other well.

When you meet another MRKH sister, you instantly bond with each other as though we're friends for a long time. The instant bonding comes from knowing we share MRKH. Our hearts connect in a compassionate, empathetic way. We are no longer strangers; we are sisters.

The meeting that day was better than I expected. Some speakers were doctors that knew all about MRKH. (In my lifetime, I'd never met one doctor that knew what MRKH was) so, this was new for me. Hearing them speak, I felt reassured that some medical people knew what MRKH is and things that can happen physically to women with MRKH. There is also the psychological aspect of MRKH. Psychologists were in attendance too.

One doctor, Dr. Mama, had his office in New Jersey. I spoke with him on one of our breaks and inquired if he'd meet with me for an appointment. I told Dr. Mama I lived in Florida; I was in my 60s and never met a doctor in my entire life that knew what MRKH was. I asked if I could set an appointment to see him. I had a lifetime of questions for him and would like him to review my medical records. He was so friendly and encouraged me to set up an appointment.

After I got home to Florida, Terry and I flew up to see Dr. Mama in December. He took two hours with us. He reviewed my medical records and examined me. For the first time in 40+ years, I had answers to my questions with MRKH. He gave me peace about my physical body for the first time in my life. What a relief!

Meeting my young MRKH sisters that day, I was impressed with their support with one or both parents attending the meet-up with their daughters.

I brought copies of my poem book to the meeting and gave everyone a copy. This day was of monumental importance. My gratitude for everyone at the meeting included special thanks to Amy, Meredith, and Christina.

Sadly, a few years later, I learned Meredith had passed away. I sobbed sorrowful tears as she was my first friend and MRKH sister for such a short time. She had the most crucial impact on my life. I am forever grateful for Meredith being my first real voice of MRKH. Her encouragement to attend the meet-up in Philadelphia was the key that unlocked my door of isolation and opened my life to freedom, sisterhood, and acceptance.

About five years later, while researching for this book, there was information about a conference in Australia called the Global MRKH Conference. I reached out to Amy Lossie and asked her about the meeting. It sounded exciting. I was considering attending with Terry. After we talked for a bit, Amy offered me an opportunity to speak at the Global MRKH. What an honor! It was both exciting and humbling. We agreed to reconnect in a week to discuss it further.

Amy put me in touch with another MRKH sister in Australia, named Kristy. She organized and set up the conference. We had phone meetings and a few Skype meetings. As I learned more of what the expectations were, we moved forward. It was a delight working with Kristy. I couldn't wait to meet her in Australia. She's extremely organized and did an outstanding job with the conference.

I also looked forward to seeing Amy, many MRKH sisters, and speaking at the conference. Going to Australia and the Global MRKH Conference was an adventure that Terry and I recall with great joy. We felt blessed to have been there and to be a part of such an important event.

I brought a second edition of, <u>The King's Poems: A Book of Faith, Hope & Love</u> to the conference. The introduction in this 2nd edition tells of my story of MRKH. I wanted this edition to be MRKH specific.

When it was my turn to speak at the conference, it was fun to hear Kristy in her pretty Australian accent introduce me. She said, "I'd now like to welcome our first international speaker, Julie Coveney. Julie traveled from Florida, U.S., to be here today. Julie was diagnosed with MRKH in 1970 and considers herself a senior ambassador for MRKH. Please welcome Julie to share her story."

Walking to the podium felt like a power surge of nerves, excitement, and Holy Spirit power! Humbled and happy, it was time to tell my story of surviving MRKH without computers for 40+ years. What a great experience to have had this opportunity.

Also, I introduced the afternoon session called Ages & Stages. In this session we'd cover what kinds of things we went through at different times of our lives with MRKH. We met in groups of women of similar age range.

I cherished sitting around the table with the MRKH sisters in my age group. We spoke of numerous experiences we had been through. Each story was unique. The most important part was that we all agreed we'd not trade our MRKH for anything. Each of us felt the life experience formed our lives in a way that nothing else could have. It was an honor to be with these brave, strong MRHK warrior sisters. It was extraordinary. In hindsight, we agreed that the process takes time, but acceptance brings healing, hope, and freedom.

After many years of silence, I decided to share my MRKH story with the world. This was possible only by:

1.) My personal relationship with Jesus Christ, gave me the courage and ability to reveal my lifelong secret.

2.) I realized sharing my testimony brought healing to myself and others.

3.) Groups like BYMRKH and meeting other MRKH women builds a community and connection. Through the numerous examples of other MRKH women, who modeled transparency through blogs, videos, and more...inspired me to share my story in hopes of encouraging others.

"As iron sharpens iron,
so one person sharpens another."

Proverbs 27:17 NIV

CONTEMPLATE & CONSIDER

❖ How is connecting to MRKH sisters helpful? Have you been to a meet-up gathering?

_____
_____
_____
_____
_____
_____
_____

❖ Why are MRKH sisters so wonderful to know and grow with?

_____
_____
_____
_____
_____
_____
_____

13

CHILDREN ACROSS THE GLOBE

Terry and I were able to take mission trips with our church. Two were to Africa and one to Israel. These mission trips were exciting and filled with unexpected blessings. One such trip was to Zimbabwe, Africa.

We now sponsor two children in Zimbabwe through a program called: One Child Matters. Part of the sponsorship is letter writing between us and the child. It is sweet to receive and read their letters. We enjoy this so much. Our financial support provides their education and meals.

At school, the children are learning English as a second language. They have someone to oversee and help them with their letter writing. They are short letters, but enough to tell us a bit of what's happening in their lives. The school they attend is through One Child Matters.

On our first trip to Zimbabwe, we had one sponsored child, named Blessed. We sponsored her for several years. We enjoyed hearing from Blessed, she wrote us letters and we'd write back. One Child Matters sends us pictures of the children. Terry and I were excited about being in Africa and meeting Blessed. We couldn't wait!

While there, one day a sweet young woman in her 20s came up to me. She had a beautiful smile, and she asked me, "Is your name Julie?"

I answered, "Yes, it is, what is your name?"

The young woman said, "My name is Talent and I help Blessed write her letters to you."

I replied with, "So it is you I've been communicating with for five years!" Talent smiled, laughed, and we both gave each other a big hug. We were happy to meet each other. I thanked Talent for helping Blessed write her beautiful letters. We always love getting them. Having sponsored her for several years, we can see her progress in maturity and writing. It's amazing.

One day of our trip, lunch was provided by Celebration Church in Zimbabwe that works with the One Child Matters Program. We'd be able to meet and have lunch with our child or children we were sponsoring. Terry and I couldn't wait to have lunch with our sponsored child, Blessed. As I said, we had been communicating with her for five years. Talent, her helper and teacher, joined us for lunch too. How nice to enjoy this special time and opportunity to be face to face with Blessed, and Talent.

On that day meeting Blessed was more special than I can describe. What a sweet girl! We knew her right away when we saw her because she had sent us pictures. Her twin brother also joined us. His name is Blessing. He had a different sponsor, but we could meet and be with him too. It was hugs, smiles and joy all around. We have cherished the memories of this day. We all had a blast. The children were great. Blessed was more beautiful than her pictures. We felt like we knew each other, even though we had just met each other for the first time.

Before we came to Africa, in the planning for the lunch and meeting with our sponsored children, we got information on sizes, needs, favorite colors, and things like that. We brought gifts of clothing, shoes, other needs they may have. We also brought fun things like toys, games, or costume jewelry. Our gifts we brought were well received. Blessed and Blessing were happy with it all.

Something took Terry and I by surprise...Blessed had a unique gift for us. She created a scrapbook consisting of letters we sent her and pictures she drew. It was beautiful. Blessed also made Terry and I bracelets with our names on them.

When we returned, on a second trip to Africa a couple of years later, we had another sponsored child named Amanda. We had a similar luncheon with her, Blessed, and Talent. Again, we had a great time together. Amanda was about the age Blessed was when we first sponsored her. We met Amanda's mom too. Each visit to Africa is very special in its own way. We enjoyed going there. The people in Africa are like family to us. We'd love to visit again.

One evening we had an African dinner at Celebration Church. It truly was a splendid night, and the people cooked in large pots outside on the church grounds. Everyone there...the African people were dressed in their pretty bright African dresses and attire. There were tables set up outside with music and candles. The atmosphere was welcoming and festive. Our meal was genuine African Cuisine. We looked forward to it and it did not disappoint; it was delicious.

Before the night began, Talent stopped by to see us. It was still daytime. She wanted to share a personal story with me.

We sat off by ourselves and she started to cry. Talent shared with me she was raised by her aunt and uncle and that she had never met her biological parents. Talent sobbed. Her greatest sorrow was not knowing her own mother and father. We were sitting at a table and we just held each other's hands tight as tears streamed down her face. I listened to her story, and she shared how sad it was for her to never have found her parents. She had spent years looking for them. I listened, asked a few questions, and then I felt led to tell Talent my MRKH story.

I told Talent that at 19 years old, never having had my period, I went to the doctor and found out that I could never have my own child or children because of MRKH. Talent cried for me too. We both shed emotional tears. I suggested we adopt each other, and on that very night, we did. We are a mom and daughter of our hearts. We hugged and felt a close connection of our new roles as mother and daughter.

From that moment on Talent and I have communicated almost daily on What's App on our phones. We both are grateful that God gave us each other. She is a very special, lovely girl. Talent is a great prayer warrior. Often, we give each other prayer requests to pray for.

She refers to Terry and me as Dad and Mom. God is so good. How could we have ever known the great plans God had in store for us? We are very grateful. In Africa we have Talent, her son Lionel, Blessed and Amanda. Our family keeps growing by the grace and goodness of God.

Terry, Julie and Talent with their two
sponsored children in Africa.

CONTEMPLATE & CONSIDER

❖ What are other ways to be involved with children in your life?

_____
_____
_____
_____
_____
_____
_____

❖ Can you consider being "motherly" to others as a benefit to you and the other?

_____
_____
_____
_____
_____
_____
_____

14

MISSION, MESSAGE AND MINISTRY

Writing this story has helped me see how God was with me in every part of my life. Even in the craziest times, He never left me. Even before I knew Him well, God knew and loved me. He knows and loves you too. Thinking about my life now, I couldn't have imagined it to be as good as it is today, compared to when I first learned of my MRKH fifty years ago! Looking back, my vision of God's love is 20/20. God knew the plans He had for me. My life isn't perfect, yet when I have trials, I'm not alone. He's with me always.

I'd like to share part of one of my favorite Psalms that comforts me as a woman with MRKH:

"You made all the delicate, inner parts of my body and knit me together in my mother's womb. Thank you for making me so wonderfully complex!

Your workmanship is marvelous - how well I know it. You watched me as I was being formed in utter seclusion, as I was woven together in the dark of the womb.

You saw me before I was born. Every day of my life was recorded in your book. Every moment was laid out before a single day had passed.

How precious are your thoughts about me, O God They cannot be numbered! I can't even count them. They outnumber the grains of sand! And when I wake up, You are still with me!"   Psalm 139: 13-18 NLT

This Psalm tells me God knew everything about every day of my life before I was born, when He saw my unformed body in my mother's womb.

God is our divine Architect before we even enter this world. He doesn't make mistakes. God is omniscient all-knowing, omnipresent all-present, and omnipotent all-powerful. I believe he knew I had MRKH before I was born. He knew why. I am comforted by His divine and perfect love and His plan for my life.

There are so many of my favorite scriptures in God's Word, the Bible. His book is truth. Did you know there are over 3000 promises in God's Word? Here are a few you may be amazed at dealing with our feelings of hurt, sorrow, barrenness, or fear.

"The LORD is close to the brokenhearted and saves those who are crushed in spirit." (Psalm 34:18 NIV)

"He settles the childless woman in her home as a happy mother of children." (Psalm 113:9 NIV)

"You turned my wailing into dancing; you removed my sackcloth and clothed me with joy, that my heart may sing your praises and not be silent. Lord, my God, I will praise you forever." (Psalm 30:11-12 NIV)

"I sought the LORD, and he answered me; he delivered me from all my fears. Those who look to him are radiant; their faces are never covered with shame." (Psalm 34: 4-5 NIV)

"I will glory in the LORD; let the afflicted hear and rejoice. Glorify the LORD with me; let us exalt his name together." (Psalm 34:2-3 NIV)

Before going to Australia to speak at the Global MRKH Conference, one morning I woke up at 4:00 a.m. with the words: Mission, Message and Ministry on my mind. When I shared this with a friend, Kristen, at church, she was excited and pointed out scripture with these words in them:

"Therefore, if anyone is in Christ, the new creation has come: The old is gone; the new is here! All this is from God, who reconciled us to himself through Christ and gave us the **ministry** *of reconciliation: that God was reconciling the world to himself in Christ, not counting people's sins against them. And he has committed to us the* **message** *of reconciliation. We are, therefore, Christ's ambassadors, as though God were making his appeal through us. We implore you on Christ's behalf: Be reconciled to God. God made him who had no sin to be sin for us so that in him we might become the righteousness of God"* (2 Corinthians 5:17-21 NIV).

It's my **mission** and privilege to share Jesus with you.

MRKH Poem

Father, you made me special with my missing part.
When I first learned of this, it broke my heart.

Why could this be? Why Me? Oh this life, I wanted to flee!
The reason unclear, I could not know.
I gave "my sadness" to You in this blow.

So unable to figure out any good reason,
Your sovereignty I learned in this difficult season.

I still don't know why, but I am sure…
I'm not to question,
You are my LORD!

You help me accept this each and every day.
I'm stronger than ever…in so many ways.

You knew all my days…before I had one.
Just like You knew…I'd be saved by Jesus, Your Son!

Our trials are treasures turned inside out.
Growing closer to You is what it's about.

Thank You for loving me and setting me apart.
I grew closer to You, right from the start.

By: Julie Coveney

EPILOGUE

Writing this book, at nearly 70 years old, my heart's desire is to help those living with MRKH or infertility issues. Motherhood for women with MRKH differs greatly from those who give birth naturally. I've seen MRKH Warrior Sister's happily share their great news and joy of adoption, or having a child via surrogacy, or even through marriage. For myself, I love my step daughters as if they were my biological children. Motherhood is surely possible, **love** is the key!

Today, I consider my MRKH a great blessing because:

MRKH taught me there is more than one way to be a mom.
MRKH brought me to God and gave me a new life in Christ.
MRKH strengthened me significantly.
MRKH produced in me an empathetic heart.
MRKH gave me MRKH sisters across the globe.
MRKH taught me patience, trust, faith, and courage.
MRKH gave me a unique perspective and path in life, for which I am forever grateful.

Writing is a form of healing. I'd like to encourage you to journal, blog, or perhaps write a book of your own. I also believe that connecting with other likeminded people, and those who understand what you're going through is essential. I've learned it is best to feel, to heal.

Thank you for reading *More Reason to Know Him.*

Care to connect? Email me at: jcfl32@yahoo.com

God Bless you,
Julie Coveney

We enjoyed sharing our story,
for His glory with you!
Terry & Julie

ADDITIONAL RESOURCES

ACOG: www.acog.org

BYMRKH: www.beautifulyoumrkh.org

NORD: rarediseases.org

The Center for Young Women's Health: (from Boston Children's Hospital) https://youngwomenshealth.org/

Alcoholics Anonymous: www.alcoholicsanonymous.org

Celebrate Recovery: www.celebraterecovery.com

Grief Share: www.griefshare.org

One Child Matters: my.onechild.org/sponsor/Zimbabwe

ABOUT THE AUTHOR

Julie Coveney lives in the sunny state of Florida with her husband, Terry, and her four legged fur baby, Teddy Bear. They enjoy getting outdoors for fresh air and walks around their neighborhood. Julie enjoys having coffee or lunch with friends and family.

Julie and Terry love traveling and seeing new places. Part of their travel includes missionary trips. They have been to Brazil, Africa, Australia, Alaska, and Israel. They also enjoy traveling back to NJ to visit family and friends.

Both, Terry and Julie, are active in their church; serving and leading small groups. More importantly, Julie loves sharing her faith and testimony with others. She believes in her heart that God has blessed her with a message, mission, and ministry, which includes being born with MRKH and sharing the Good News of Christ.

You can reach Julie at: jcfl32@yahoo.com

OTHER BOOKS BY JULIE COVENEY

The King's Poems: From
God's Heart to Yours
ISBN: 9781499693928

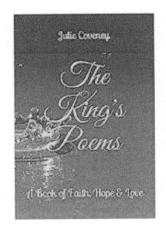

The King's Poems: A Book
of Faith, Hope & Love
ISBN: 9781698835693

Made in the USA
Monee, IL
18 July 2025

21015769R00075